Dissent in Three American Wars

Samuel Eliot Morison
Frederick Merk
Frank Freidel

Harvard University Press
Cambridge, Massachusetts
1970

Distributed in Great Britain by Oxford University Press, London
Library of Congress catalog card number 74-105373
SBN 674-21278-9
Printed in the United States of America

Chapter 1, by Samuel Eliot Morison, contains, in condensed form, much material from Chapters 16, 17, and 18 of his book, *Harrison Gray Otis, 1765–1848: The Urbane Federalist* (Boston, Houghton Mifflin, 1969), and is included here with the permission of Houghton Mifflin Company.

Contents

Illustrations

Foreword

The essays printed in this volume were originally presented in 1968–69 as a series of evening lectures at the Massachusetts Historical Society. "Dissent in Three American Wars" was chosen as the subject of the series to remind our audience that disagreement was a phenomenon of the other wars in which this nation has engaged and is not restricted to America's unpopular involvement in the Vietnam struggle. It was decided not to include the better-known examples of the American Revolution and the Civil War but to focus attention on three smaller conflicts—the War of 1812, the Mexican War, and the Spanish-American War with the Philippine Insurrection. Three of the Society's most distinguished members (all of Harvard University)—Samuel Eliot Morison, Jonathan Trumbull Professor of American History, Emeritus; Frederick Merk, Gurney Professor of History and Political Science, Emeritus; and Frank Burt Freidel, Jr., Professor of History—delivered lectures which were received so enthusiastically that it was obvious they should be printed for a wider audience.

STEPHEN T. RILEY, *Director*
Massachusetts Historical Society

1

Samuel Eliot Morison

Dissent in the War of 1812

In working over sources for my *Harrison Gray Otis, Urbane Federalist* (1969) I was astonished to find how little work had been done on the internal history of the War of 1812 since my *Harrison Gray Otis, Federalist* came out in 1913. Plenty of books there have been on the causes of the war, and a few good articles on its military, naval, and diplomatic history, but nothing of any consequence on political, economic, or other internal matters during the war. It has generally been assumed that Henry Adams had said the last word on those aspects. My second biography of Otis includes an attempt to set forth some of the anti-war trends in Massachusetts, especially the potentially dangerous "Reunion of the Original Thirteen States" movement promoted by John Lowell.

In my opinion the most unpopular war that this country has ever waged, not even excepting the Vietnam conflict, was our second war with Great Britain. The declaration on June 18, 1812, passed by only 79 to 49 in the House, and 19 to 13 in the Senate. Eight out of ten New England senators, eleven out of fourteen New York representatives, voted against it. Although the South and West in general were keen for the war, their enthusiasm did not last. The War Department could never build up the regular army to half its authorized strength and obtained only 10,000 one-year volunteers out of 50,000 authorized. Henry Clay boasted that he could conquer Canada with Kentucky militia alone, but Kentucky furnished only 400 recruits in 1812. Thomas

Jefferson said that the conquest of Canada would be only a matter of marching—but it turned out to be a matter of fighting as well, since the Canadians, French as well as British, instead of "rising as one man" to "throw off the British yoke" (as the Secretary of War, William Eustis of Roxbury, Massachusetts, predicted), showed a perverse disposition to fight for King and Country. Interestingly enough, the loyal minority in New England more than made up for the discouraging stand of the Federalist state governments; those five states provided the regular army with nineteen regiments as against fifteen from the middle states and ten from the southern states.

After Hull's surrender of Detroit in 1812 had shown that the war would be no walkover, it became heartily disliked throughout the country. You might say that it was our most popular war when it was over and our most unpopular while it lasted.

The notion that only Yankee Federalists opposed the war is pure myth. Robert Smith, a Maryland merchant-shipowner who served in Jefferson's and Madison's cabinets, issued a public address against the war and sent a copy to Chief Justice Marshall, who replied in part: "All minor considerations should be waived . . . and the great division between the friends of peace & the advocates of war ought alone to remain. . . . All who wish peace ought to unite in the means which may facilitate its attainment." Senator Beveridge, Marshall's biographer, admits that the chief justice opposed the war as bitterly as did Harrison Gray Otis or Timothy Pickering and that most of the southern Federalists were of the same mind. But the Yankee Federalists called down most of the postwar odium on themselves because they alone controlled state governments and were able to turn state rights against the nation.

After Congress declared war, the lower house of the Massachusetts General Court issued an address to the people, saying, "Organize a *peace party* throughout your Country, and let all other party distinctions vanish." Governor Caleb Strong followed this up by proclaiming a public fast to atone for a declaration of war "against the nation from which we are descended, and which for many generations has been the bulwark of the religion we profess."

The war slogan of the administration, "Free Trade and Sailors' Rights," seemed mere hokum to Federalists and to the shipowning community generally; they were making big money in neutral trade, and the number of impressments of native-born American seamen was small. Fundamentally, it seemed wicked and unchristian to Federalists to attack England when she was "the world's last hope" against the tyrant Napoleon. As Harrison Gray Otis wrote, "The most intelligent and respectable men in the country . . . tremble for the prosperity and fate of Britain, and consider her . . . as the Bulwark of the liberties of this country and mankind." That belief happened to be correct in 1812. Napoleon had suppressed every vestige of liberty in Western Europe save in England, Portugal, and recalcitrant Spain. Within a week after America declared war on Great Britain, his grand army entered Russia. England's cause in 1812, as in 1914 and 1939, was that of the free world.

Certain old and important Republican families of Massachusetts, such as Adams, Gerry, Austin, and Crowninshield, supported the war; but most of the old families were anti-war Federalists. The Harvard Corporation—President Kirkland, Treasurer Davis, Fellows Lathrop, Lowell, Phillips, Gore, and Chauncey—was 100 percent anti-war. This they publicly proclaimed at Commencement in 1814 by conferring honorary degrees on John Lowell, the secessionist; H. G. Otis, leader of the New England Convention movement; Judge Isaac Parker, who advised Governor Strong to withhold militia; and Chief Justice Tilghman of Pennsylvania, who had defied the federal government in the Olmstead case.[1]

The Massachusetts Federalists maintained a policy of giving the war minimum support consistent with obedience to the laws (as interpreted by themselves) in the hope of promoting a speedy peace. Governor Strong decided whether to honor presidential requisitions for militia, and refused most of them. So did every other New England governor except Gilman of New Hampshire. There was a certain justification for this localism.[2] In July 1812, almost every regular unit garrisoning coastal forts marched off to invade Canada, leaving the New England coast defenseless except for militia. Distrustful as the state administrations were of the Washington government, they refused requisitions not merely to spite the "little man in the Palace," as they called President Madison,[3] but because the militia, who elected their own

1. For the Olmstead case, see a valuable and much neglected work, Herman V. Ames, *State Documents on Federal Relations* (Philadelphia, 1906), 45–52.

2. See Ames, 54–64, for the constitutional side of this contest between the New England states and the federal government.

3. It is a curious human trait to avoid mentioning by name someone you bitterly hate. Most of us remember Franklin D. Roosevelt's being called "That man [*or:* That ————————] in the White House"; and, a generation earlier, the editor of a New York newspaper gave orders to his staff never to mention the name of Theodore Roosevelt.

officers, balked at being placed under officers of the regular army. General Winfield Scott of Virginia wrote in his *Memoirs* what nobody dared to say during the war, that Madison refused commissions to Federalist gentlemen who wanted to serve, and in New England "there were but very few educated Republicans." Hence the Yankees selected for commissions "consisted mostly of coarse and ignorant men. In the other States . . . the appointments consisted, generally, of swaggerers, dependants, decayed gentlemen and others fit for nothing else, which always turned out *utterly unfit for any military purpose whatsoever.*"

Boston Federalists condescended to celebrate American naval victories, since they regarded the United States Navy as a Federalist creation which the Jeffersonians had starved and neglected. A naval ball at the Exchange Coffee House on State Street in March 1813 was the only public function during the war when both parties got together. There was dancing from 8:00 to 11:00, and "a sumptuous supper," at which seven hundred were able to sit down at once. As the Boston *New England Palladium* reported: "The splendor of the ball was never equalled in this town, and we believe never was surpassed in the United States. Commodores Rodgers and Bainbridge and Capt. Hull, with their respective ladies . . . and most of the other naval officers in town, augmented the brilliancy, as much as they increased the enjoyments of the evening."

A service of plate was presented by Boston to Commodore Oliver H. Perry after his victory on Lake Erie, but, according to the diary of the Rev. William Bentley, "Commodore Perry passed through Salem this day towards Portsmouth. No notice was given of his visit and no ceremonies passed."

Salem, Newburyport, and Essex County generally (always excepting Marblehead!) were solidly anti-war. The Republican press reported that a five-star, five-stripe flag was displayed by the Sea Fencibles of Newburyport and that a mob there tried to liberate British prisoners brought in by the privateer *Grand Turk.*

In celebrating American naval victories, the Boston Federalists spent far less energy and enthusiasm than over two European events, the retreat of Napoleon from Moscow, and the entrance of the Allies into Paris. The festivities to celebrate the Russian victory opened on March 25, 1813 in King's Chapel. A choir sang Handel's *Hallelujah Chorus,* the Rev. William Ellery Channing offered a prayer which "united the elegance, and what the French call the *onction* of Fénelon, with the simplicity of the Apostolick Age," and the Rev. James Freeman delivered an extraordinary discourse composed of passages from the Old Testament so cunningly woven together as to appear a prophecy of recent events. Harrison Gray Otis presided at a public dinner in the Exchange Coffee House, where President Kirkland of Harvard invoked the Lord's blessing. At the first toast, to "Alexander the Great," a transparency representing the Emperor as "The Deliverer of Europe" was unveiled, an orchestra played the imperial Russian anthem, and everyone rose and cheered.

Similarly, in 1814, Boston sang no hallelujahs for Macdonough's naval victory on Lake Champlain but held a "Splendid and Solemn Festival" on June 15 to commemorate the "downfall of the Tyrant" Napoleon. In the evening the State House was illuminated, a band played in the colonnade, red-hot shot and "carbonic comets" were fired from Boston Neck, and the John Hancock mansion was adorned with transparencies showing fleurs-de-lys and "Honor to the Allies." We were then supposed to be fighting the principal ally, England.

Celebrations of this sort were not confined to Boston, or even to New England. The New York Federalists had them too, and John Randolph of Roanoke wrote to Josiah Quincy declaring that Boston had done herself proud.

Whatever Boston Federalists were able to effect by resolutions and celebrations paled in comparison with the results of their financial policy. Various factors resulting from the war gave New England a monopoly of manufactured and imported goods, and a large part of the specie in the country migrated to Boston banks. These institutions, with one exception, were controlled by Federalists, and Philadelphia financial circles were similarly constituted. A good understanding existed between the financial powers of Philadelphia and Boston (New York, apparently, did not count) to withhold subscriptions to government loans until assured of peace, hoping thus to force President Madison to abandon his strategy of conquering Canada. And they nearly succeeded in bankrupting their government at a very critical period.

On April 4, 1814 Congress authorized a new loan of $25 million. Otis and the Philadelphia bankers David Parish and Charles Willing Hare were eager to subscribe. Money had become plentiful in both cities and hard to place; Washington would get the money somehow; they hated to miss an opportunity for safe and lucrative investment. The Philadelphians argued that subscribing to loans was no greater encouragement of the war than paying customs duties on imports and pointed out that Federalists would not be exempt from the baleful consequences of a collapse of the government and a total prostration of public credit. The leading merchant-financiers of Boston, including George Cabot, John Phillips, Samuel Eliot, Theodore Lyman, and Thomas Handasyd Perkins, thrashed the matter out at a private meeting. Otis argued the Philadelphia case but Cabot countered (so he wrote to Otis five years later) "on the ground that the war was *absolutely unjust*"; hence "we ought never to *volunteer* our services in a cause which we believe to be morally wrong." The meeting then voted to help the government financially only upon receiving definite assurances from Washington that satisfactory instructions had been given to the peace commissioners. Like any self-respecting government, it refused to give this information, and the loan proved a failure without Federalist support. Boston took up only $1 million of the loan; but Virginia, a state which shouted most loudly for the war, subscribed only $200,000.

By the close of 1813, another act of government enhanced the woes of maritime New England. Contraband trade, especially in Maine and Georgia, had assumed such proportions that Congress passed a general embargo act even more severe than Jefferson's, prohibiting all coasting trade and fishing outside harbors. "Madison's Embargo" aroused the most indignant protests in eastern Maine, where the only way to get about was by water. The voters of Deer Isle passed resolutions denouncing Madison's embargo as "the utmost stench of despotism"; Belfast declared that the sufferings, injuries, and oppressions "under the present Dynasty are tenfold greater" than those of 1775–76; Ellsworth compared Madison to Bonaparte; the voters of Gouldsborough complained that even sleighs carrying food for their families were stopped and searched for contraband by Madison's minions; Castine asked, "Shall Massachusetts be... obliged to carry on this war forever to gratify the malignity of a few individuals directed by 'an unseen hand'?"—Napoleon, of course. Maine was the hottest part of the antiwar bloc in 1813–14.[4] Cyrus King, brother to Rufus King, ran for Congress from a Maine district and won, on an extremist platform. In a widely quoted speech he said, "If a simple king of England, by his corrupt servants, chastised New England with whips, the administration here chastised her with scorpions. . . . The states of New England can never be satellites."

Only because moderate Federalist leaders such as Otis, Josiah Quincy, and James Lloyd acted as brakes did the Massachusetts General Court avoid confrontation with the Union during the winter session of 1813–14. Senator Timothy Pickering, stung by the sneers of his Washington colleagues that Massachusetts might bluster but dared not act, spurred on his followers. Francis Blake, state senator from Worcester, delivered a glowing eulogy of Great Britain, declaring that if our Constitution permitted embargoes, he preferred the British, "monarchy and all." Samuel Fessenden of New Gloucester, Maine, announced that "it was time to take our rights into our own hands. . . . We ought to establish a custom house by law, and the sooner we come at issue with the general government the better." One who heard this speech wrote that "these ravings of a political maniac were received with manifest applause." But, he adds, Harrison Gray Otis threw cold water upon them.

4. These town resolutions are in the Massachusetts Archives (State House, Boston).

By the spring of 1814, so violent had become the feeling against war and embargo that Massachusetts Republicans dared not go before the people on a platform of unqualified support of the war and the administration. They nominated for governor Samuel Dexter, who in an open letter proclaimed himself still a Federalist, announced that on the policy of commercial restriction he "differs radically from the party called Republican, and *he desires that they should know it*," and that his only quarrel with the Federalists arose from their aggressive pacifism. Caleb Strong won his tenth election easily; and, more significant, 360 Federalists and only 156 Republicans were elected to the lower house of the General Court.

Presently there developed a situation even more critical and alarming to New England than before. The British government, relieved in Europe by the collapse of Napoleon's empire, prepared to overwhelm its only remaining enemy by invasions and raids at every vulnerable point of the American coast and frontier. Hitherto New England had not been invested by sea, but in June 1814 British men-of-war blockaded her ports and began minor raiding attacks on several points along our coast. On July 7, armed barges from a warship off Boston Light raided the harbor and carried off five small sloops. Moose Island and Eastport, Maine, were captured on July 11, and the inhabitants were required to take an oath of allegiance to King George. On August 30–31 Boston learned details of the Battle of Bladensburg, the capture of Washington, and the burning of the Capitol. On September 4 Sir George Prevost invaded New York at Lake Champlain with the finest British army ever sent to America. On the same day it became known in Boston that a formidable naval expedition (three ships of the line, two frigates, three more warships, and ten transports lifting 3,500 soldiers) under Lieutenant General Sherbrook had occupied Castine, raided Bangor, and taken possession of eastern Maine. Almost everyone assumed that Sherbrook would next attack Boston.

With the federal government a fugitive from Washington, national integrity threatened at every point, the regular army undermined by desertion, and several states forced to provide for their own defense, the Union has never been so weak, or national prestige so low, as in that first week of September 1814.

The war department did indeed offer to undertake the recovery of Castine and eastern Maine, if Massachusetts would undertake to furnish troop-lift for 5,000 men, raise them, feed and pay them, to be reimbursed after the war. Governor Strong refused, as no such expedition was militarily feasible. With the entire New England coast blockaded by the enemy, no armed ship could even get at the British in Castine, where no fewer than fourteen ships of the Royal Navy were constantly maintained, and where several thousand redcoats garrisoned Fort George and nearby redoubts. Strong well remembered the futile, disastrous attempt to recapture Castine during the War of Independence; and he pointed out that without a superior naval force—and most of the ships of the United States were then blockaded in harbor—any such attempt in 1814 would be doomed to certain defeat and merely expose the inhabitants to violent reprisals.[5]

5. George A. Wheeler, *Castine Past and Present* (Boston, 1896) blames Strong; anyone who reads Mahan's account of naval events in 1814 will endorse the Governor's wisdom. Cf. Richard Hildreth, *The History of the United States of America*, 6 vols. (New York, 1876), VI, 538, who

As a result of this startling series of events in the summer of 1814, Governor Strong summoned the already elected General Court for a special session on October 5. In his opening speech the governor described the state's situation in the most gloomy terms. His speech was referred to a joint committee of which H. G. Otis was chairman. "Otis's Report," submitted in three days' time, exhorted all citizens to unite "in repelling our invading foe," but deplored "the destructive policy by which a state of unparalleled national felicity has been converted into one of humiliation, of danger, and distress." He recommended that a convention of the New England states be summoned immediately, to deal with the grievances of that section and to do something about local defense.

Otis's Report became the subject of a long-winded, acrimonious debate in the General Court. "Monarchy and all" Blake proposed to prohibit the federal government from collecting duties, excises, or other taxes in Massachusetts. Otis declared he was "extremely sorry for this," believed it to be "very injurious to our national government," and persuaded the Worcester senator, much against his will, to withdraw his motion. Leverett Saltonstall, the young member from Salem, made an able speech defending Governor Strong's stand on the militia problem. He attempted to answer the charge of poor timing at a period of national peril by quoting 2 Corinthians 6 : 2: "Now is the accepted time; behold, now

---

adds that the selection of General Henry Dearborn to head this dubious enterprise was considered "a deliberate insult." Nobody has yet written a candid history of eastern Maine under this British occupation. From what I can gather, the people at large welcomed it as an alternative to the embargoes, etc., of the Madison administration and made good money trading with Nova Scotia.

1. Harrison Gray Otis. Portrait by Chester Harding.

is the day of salvation." Saltonstall admitted the Union to be in danger, but that was not New England's fault. Unless *we* make an effort, the Union "will soon as naturally fall asunder, as ripe fruit falling from our trees."[6] John Holmes of Maine, ablest orator on the Republican side, answered Saltonstall in a speech that took two and a half hours to deliver and in which he called Otis "the flippant orator, the pretty man." Nevertheless, Otis's Report passed the state senate on October 12 by a vote of 22 to 12 and passed the house four days later by 260 to 20. A letter of invitation was sent to the other New England state governors to be represented at Hartford, and those of Rhode Island and Connecticut promptly accepted.

Exactly what was the Hartford Convention expected to accomplish? The official objectives were to draft constitutional amendments to protect New England interests and to agree with the federal government to let the states conduct their own defense. But was that really all? John Quincy Adams and the Republicans charged that the whole thing was a secession plot, to be initiated by concluding a separate peace with Great Britain. We may confidently deny that charge, since all evidence points to the fact that Otis, George Cabot, and their colleagues wished to avoid secession at any cost; but anti-war sentiment had gone very, very far indeed.

That fall, Congressmen who had voted for the war were bawled at as "war hawks" and hustled on the streets of Boston and Plymouth. And at the congressional elections in

6. Boston *Weekly Messenger*, Nov. 18, 1814. I consulted this and other newspapers of 1814 at the Boston Athenæum and the Massachusetts Historical Society.

early November every district in Massachusetts proper, and six out of seven in Maine, elected an anti-war Federalist candidate. Even Joseph Varnum's safe Middlesex district, despite a ringing appeal by Samuel Hoar and John Keyes to show its "indignation" over the Hartford Convention, went Federalist. Even John Holmes of Maine, the Republican leader in the General Court, went down to defeat. Never had the Federalists enjoyed so nearly a clean sweep. A writer in the Republican Boston *Patriot* of December 7 admitted that at least half the people of Massachusetts were for disunion and warned that if it came to that the Bay State, ruled by "Blakes, Quincys, Pickerings and Saltonstalls," would have to live off the export of "potash, mules, grindstones and pine boards." And an earthquake shock on November 30, first to be felt in Boston since 1783, convinced many of the godly that the Almighty intended to give the "Headquarters of Good Principles" a good shaking-up.

Most of the proposals which Otis and Cabot regarded as dangerous, and which they hoped would whistle out to sea when the Convention met, were for seizing customs houses, impounding federal revenues, declaring neutrality, nullifying conscription,[7] and the like. Such action would certainly have brought a direct confrontation between state and federal governments, which Otis and other moderate Federalists wished above all to avoid.

One threat which they knew nothing about was Governor

7. There was a tremendous uproar in New England over the conscription bill of Senator Giles of Virginia, which failed to pass, and over his bill to allow the enlistment of boys under eighteen without their parent's consent, which did pass. The Connecticut legislature threatened to nullify it if the administration attempted to enforce it. Ames, *State Documents*, 76.

Strong's secret mission to lay the grounds for an armistice, or separate peace, with Great Britain. This intrigue seems to have been the personal diplomacy of the supposedly simple, straightforward sage of Northampton, whose speeches had been published under the title *Piety and Patriotism*. Canny Caleb was too cagey to put anything down in writing, but he sent Thomas Adams, Federalist member of the General Court from occupied Castine, to General Sir John Sherbrooke at Halifax in mid-November 1814 with oral instructions to ascertain the "views" of the British government in the event of a direct clash between himself and Madison. Sir John wrote to Lord Bathurst, the Colonial Secretary, on November 20 that he hoped His Majesty's government would profit from any such opportunity to break up the American Union. Bathurst replied from London on December 13, 1814, that if Madison did not ratify the peace treaty, which he expected would shortly be signed (and was signed on Christmas Eve), and the war went on, Sir John had authority to sign an armistice with the New England states and to furnish them with logistic support to help defend themselves from the expected "resentment of the American Executive." But he must not promise troops.[8]

Politically, the most dangerous element in the situation was the movement for a new union of the original thirteen states only, initiated by John Lowell.

8. The British documents on Caleb Strong's mission are in the *American Historical Review*, 43 (1938), 553–566; see also Massachusetts Historical Society, *Proceedings*, LXIX (1947–1950), 218, note 25. No name is mentioned, and the governor gave the man no credentials; but as Sir John Sherbrooke describes him as a well-known citizen of eastern Maine and a member of the General Court, I infer that Thomas Adams, representative of Castine, was the man. One of the Republican newspapers of Boston in late 1814 has a squib about Adams crossing the British lines concealed in a double-bottomed wagon.

2. Caleb Strong, governor of Massachusetts, portrayed by James B. Marston in 1807.

"Jack" Lowell was one of the most able, attractive, and imprudent of the Federalist leaders. Son of Judge John Lowell, first of that distinguished family to move to Boston from Newburyport, and of Sarah Higginson, he married Rebecca Amory; his half-brother Frances C. Lowell, whose mother was a Cabot, married a Jackson; there you have the nucleus of the famous Essex Junto. As John T. Morse, Jr., wrote, Cabots, Lowells, Lees, Jacksons, and Higginsons "knew each other well in Essex County and had a satisfying belief that New England morality and intellectuality had produced nothing better than they were; so they . . . intermarried very much, with a sure and cheerful faith that in such alliances there could be no blunders."[9] There certainly was no blunder in this case. Jack's only son John Amory Lowell married (1) his cousin Susanna Jackson and (2) his cousin Elizabeth Cabot Putnam; from them A. Lawrence Lowell, Percival Lowell, Amy Lowell, Ralph Lowell, and McGeorge Bundy are descended.

Jack Lowell was a man of wealth and of public spirit, a founder of the Massachusetts General Hospital, the Athenæum, and other old Boston institutions; and his son John Amory Lowell became the No. 1 trustee of the famous Lowell Institute. In the pretty, rural scenery of Roxbury, John Lowell had a country estate famous for horticulture and hospitality. In every aspect of life except the political, Lowell was altogether admirable; but in politics he justified nicknames applied by the local Jeffersonians: "Crazy Jack" or "The Boston Rebel."

After writing two of the most powerful anti-administration

9. *Memoir of Colonel Henry Lee* (Boston, 1905), 9.

3. John Lowell, author of the plan for a new union of the thirteen original states only. Portrait by Gilbert Stuart in 1824.

pamphlets—*Mr. Madison's War* and *Perpetual War, the Policy of Mr. Madison*—accusing the President of refusing any reasonable peace settlement, Jack Lowell furthered a proposal so idiotic that it would hardly be worth serious consideration had it not been seriously promoted in the Federalist press. It amounted to a pistol-point reorganization of the Union. He announced it in a now very rare pamphlet of 1813, *Thoughts in a Series of Letters, in Answer to a Question respecting the Division of the States*, by a Massachusetts Farmer.[10]

Lowell's plan was this: the New England Convention should draft a new federal constitution so drawn as to safeguard maritime, commercial, and New England interests. This new constitution should be presented as an ultimatum to the original thirteen states only. In other words, kick the West out of the Union!

Lowell argued that the Louisiana Purchase violated "the great original compact,"[11] bringing in a horde of ignorant congressmen determined "to prostrate our commerce." He compared the old thirteen states to a benevolent merchant with a large family who took into his house a needy stranger.

10. Copy in the Massachusetts Historical Society. No place or date on the pamphlet, the substance of which probably first appeared in a Federalist newspaper, but I have not found it. The only reference I have seen to it in any secondary work is in John S. Barry, *The History of Massachusetts*, 3 vols. (Boston, 1857), III, 419, note 3. It is attributed to Lowell in Ralph R. Shaw and Richard H. Shoemaker, *American Bibliography, Preliminary Checklist for 1813* (New York, 1962), 262 (which locates copies in seven other institutions), and there are so many phrases identical with those of Lowell's earlier pamphlets that there can be no doubt of his authorship.

11. The compact theory of the Federal Constitution, even the very words of the Virginia and Kentucky Resolves of 1798, were continually being thrown in the teeth of the Republicans by the Federalist newspapers; and Frank Maloy Anderson argued in his "Forgotten Phase" article (Mississippi Valley Historical Association, *Proceedings*, VI [1912–13], 176–188) that this was a deliberate attempt to ripen secessionist sentiment.

Pol.

PERPETUAL WAR,

THE POLICY OF MR. MADISON.

BEING A CANDID EXAMINATION OF HIS LATE MESSAGE TO CONGRESS, SO FAR AS RESPECTS THE FOLLOWING TOPICKS....VIZ.

THE PRETENDED NEGOTIATIONS FOR PEACE.....THE IMPORTANT AND INTERESTING SUBJECT OF A

CONSCRIPT MILITIA....

AND

THE ESTABLISHMENT OF AN IMMENSE STANDING ARMY OF GUARDS AND SPIES, UNDER THE NAME OF

A LOCAL VOLUNTEER FORCE.

" *Tum " Jacobus Madison secundum Præses"....gravior remediis quam delicta erant, suarumque legum auctor idem, ac subversor quæ armis tuebatur, armis amisit."* TACITI ANNALIUM LIB. III.

LIBERALLY TRANSLATED

" Then James Madison, a second time President, adopted a remedy for the wrongs of our *seamen*, infinitely more injurious to them than the evils which they suffered.....he ordered out the militia, in contempt of that very Constitution of which he was one of the principal framers. In short, whatever he attempted to vindicate by arms, by arms he lost."

[By John Lowell.]

BY A NEW-ENGLAND FARMER.

AUTHOR OF A LATE PAMPHLET, ENTITLED, " MR. MADISON'S WAR."

BOSTON :

Printed by Chester Stebbins.

....

1812.

4. One of John Lowell's anti-administration pamphlets, published in 1812.

This man "began to usurp authority . . . and succeeded so well (his host being a peaceable man)" as to persuade him to take in three or four more comrades, farmers, and moonshiners, who insisted on their host's giving up his proper business and joining them in growing corn and distilling whiskey! Whilst a separation of the West "*must* take place, and the sooner the better," Lowell hoped we might "soon again embrace our elder sister Virginia." The Westerners hate Great Britain, hate commerce, hate New England, and the Navy is an "object of their implacable hatred." We can never recover our ancient prosperity while they wield the lash. And he concludes that to unite "the original thirteen states . . . appears to be the last hope of our country."

Lowell predicted in a letter to Pickering that the eight eastern states outside New England would dare not interfere. As for pro-war Yankee Republicans, Lowell fatuously assumed that they would go along in order to be relieved from paying Madison's war taxes!

Senator Timothy Pickering in Congress took up the idea with enthusiasm, as did Gouverneur Morris of New York and Charles Carroll of Maryland. Assuming that General Pakenham's expeditionary force would defeat Andrew Jackson's army, Pickering wrote, "From the moment that the British possess New Orleans, the Union is severed." The West would embrace British sovereignty—or at least protection—to secure a Mississippi outlet, as it had often threatened to do in the past, and the rest of the original thirteen would be forced to join New England on New England's terms.

This wild scheme cannot be dismissed as a personal aberration of "Crazy Jack." Every Federalist newspaper of Boston but one promoted it as a platform for the Hartford Convention.[12] The Boston *Gazette* predicted in its number of November 17 that by July 4, 1815, "If James Madison is not out of office, a new form of government will be in operation in the eastern section of the Union." The *Columbian Centinel*, oldest and most respectable of the Boston Federalist press, promoted Lowell's scheme in a series of violent articles called "The Crisis"; and, before they were finished, started another series by a writer who chose the pseudonym "Epaminondas"—the Theban general who had detached several states from the Athenian Confederacy. "Epaminondas" urged the Hartford Convention "not to be entangled by the cobwebs of a compact which has long since ceased to exist." He declared that the Union, once a blessing, had under Madison become a curse; that New England was not afraid of secession—look at how a little country, Holland, "threw off the yoke of Spain (our Virginia)."[13]

Already on November 9 the *Centinel* had announced Connecticut's and Rhode Island's acceptance of the invitation to Hartford as "Second" and "Third Pillar of a New Federal Edifice Raised," accompanying the text by a cut showing three columns, with room for a couple more. Thus in 1788 the *Centinel* had announced successive state ratifications of the federal Constitution. A witty writer in the Republican *Yankee* for December 9 said that the *Centinel's* three pillars looked like snuff bottles in an apothecary's window; so for good Republicans the Hartford conclave became the "Snuff Bottle Convention."

On November 26 the *Centinel* sketched out a whole scheme of action for the Hartford Convention "to do to save

12. I have not, however, examined the *Repertory*.
13. *Columbian Centinel*, Dec. 21–28, 1814.

the country." "The bond of union is already broken by you, Mr. Madison." No more federal taxes should be paid until our just claims are heard. Conclude a separate peace with Great Britain to which the other states will be invited to adhere. Call a new federal convention of Northern States *only* to form a new federal constitution, which the South Atlantic States *alone* will be invited to join.[14]

And this scheme had some support outside New England, even from the press. The *Federal Republican* of Georgetown, D.C., printed an open letter to President Madison in early November: "Do immediate justice to all the reasonable claims of New England," it said. "Withdraw . . . your disgraced and incompetent generals." New England "has been driven off by every species of oppression. . . . Do you imagine that a people thus injured, insulted, abused and libelled, can possibly feel towards you any sentiment but that of deep and fixed detestation?"[15]

In the midst of all this excitement, life went on much as usual in Boston. There is a notice in the *Centinel* of December 12, 1814: "The Cotillion Party will meet at Concert-Hall on the evening of Tuesday the 15th at 6.30. H. Codman, Secretary."

Why, then, after all this fulminating, did nothing happen? Because the state legislatures had taken care to appoint to the Hartford Convention only moderate men, like George Cabot, Joseph Lyman, H. G. Otis, and Benjamin Hazard. John Lowell, in a letter to Pickering, denounced these members as timid and time-serving; not one really strong char-

14. Quoted from "Refederator" articles in the Boston *Daily Advertiser*. "Refederator" I believe to have been John Lowell.

15. Quoted in the Boston *Gazette*, Nov. 10, 1814.

acter, he said, had been sent to Hartford. And, as he feared, the Convention issued a moderate, statesmanlike Report condemning violent action. "To attempt upon every abuse of power to change the Constitution would be to perpetuate the evils of revolution," said the Report. The main cause of New England's woes has been the "fierce passions which have convulsed the nations of Europe," entering "the bosoms of our citizens"; with Napoleon's fall these should subside. And the war has proved to the interior states the value of maritime power.

But the war was still going on when the Convention adjourned on January 5, 1815 (news of the Peace of Ghent, signed on Christmas Eve, did not reach the United States until February 13). So Governor Strong appointed a committee consisting of H. G. Otis, William Sullivan, and Thomas Handasyd Perkins to go to Washington and persuade the Madison administration to hand over federal funds for the defense of Massachusetts against the enemy. That, too, had been recommended by the Hartford Convention. Nowadays, nobody thinks twice of efforts to obtain federal funds for local use; but this unprecedented effort was denounced as treasonable. The loyal Republicans got out an amusing cartoon of the three respectable gentlemen sailing to Washington in a vessel built on the lines of a chamber pot, flying a five-striped ensign with the cross of St. George in the canton. Otis is saying, "Damn me, Tom, she's sprung a leak!" To which Perkins replies, "Who's afraid? Did you ever know a ship like ours fill from her *own* bottom?"

News of the Peace of Ghent and the Battle of New Orleans, arriving in Washington exactly when the "three ambassadors" did, rendered their mission futile and ridiculous.

A curious view of this mission, to the effect that its object was to promote the secession of New England, was given by President Lyndon B. Johnson in his press conference of November 17, 1967. The President is reported[16] to have said:

"There has always been confusion, frustration, and differences of opinion when there is a war going on. . . . That was true when all of New England came down to secede in Madison's administration in the War of 1812, and stopped in Baltimore. They didn't quite make it because Andrew Jackson's results in New Orleans came in.

"They were having a party there that night. The next morning they came and told the President they wanted to congratulate him—that they thought he was right all along, although they had come from Boston to Baltimore in a secessionist mood."

Pathetic indeed. President Johnson, comparing himself wistfully with President Madison at lowest ebb, hoped that a spectacular victory like General Jackson's would shortly bring peace, so that by Christmas the "hawks" could triumph over the "doves." Alas, there was to be no Peace of Christmas Eve 1967, or 1968 either.

A myth of a New England secession plot's having been thwarted by the Treaty of Ghent and General Jackson's victory was started by administration organs almost immediately, as a smoke screen to cover Madison's mismanagement of the war. This myth, although shown to be false by every serious historian of the United States for the last 150 years, is

16. Boston *Globe*, Nov. 18, 1967; and, on the 27th, letter by me deferentially correcting this extraordinary theory of events—Otis, under whose leadership the Hartford Convention had rejected secession before it adjourned on January 5, arriving in Washington to demand secession on February 14!

5. The New England delegation to Washington is ridiculed in this Republican cartoon of 1815, which shows (left to right) Thomas Handasyd Perkins, Harrison Gray Otis, and William Sullivan in a vessel resembling a chamber pot. The words attributed to Perkins and Otis are quoted on page 27. Sullivan is saying, "Keep the flag up Harry, you was'nt born to be drown'd—sink or swim, there's no flinching now." The cartoon is part of a broadside which also contains ten stanzas of verse headed "A Trip to Washington City," to be sung to the tune of "Johnny Bull Beware."

so pleasing to people who dislike New England that many to this day continue to believe it. Presumably, President Johnson imbibed it from his school history in Texas.

We may amuse ourselves, at this safe distance, by discussing what might have happened if the war had continued well into 1815. It does not unduly strain the imagination to predict that if Madison's administration had been stubborn about ratifying the Treaty of Ghent, a very serious situation would have arisen. As a result of Governor Strong's secret diplomacy, the British authorities at Halifax had the green light from London to intervene if Madison refused to ratify the treaty, and if the New England states asked for help. Halifax was given permission to conclude an armistice with New England; and, in the event that those states were invaded by federal forces, to provide them with logistic support. There would have been a civil war, with Yankee militia supported by the Royal Navy, Canadian militia, and perhaps a fresh British expeditionary force.

Of course this is pure fantasy. Remembering the haste with which both governments ratified the Treaty of Ghent, and the fact that the British recalled General Pakenham's expeditionary force from Louisiana without even knowing whether it had won or lost, it is clear that the Peace of Christmas Eve 1814 was inevitable. And peace caused the entire sectional movement in New England, based as it was on false premises, to collapse. Everyone of both parties rejoiced over the end of this unpopular war, and New England "rebels" turned their minds to other topics.

Jack Lowell now employed his polemical pen to attack the conservatives in religion. His pamphlet *Are You a Christian or a Calvinist?* started a controversy that convulsed the Congregational churches of New England and led to the secession of orthodox churches from those that had gone liberal.

So ended the most unpopular war in our history. But because of Jackson's victory at New Orleans, the American people came to believe that they had won it, and that whatever setbacks had occurred were the fault of those nasty New England Federalists.

2

Frederick Merk

Dissent in the Mexican War

On a Monday morning—May 11, 1846—President James K. Polk sent to Congress a special message announcing war with Mexico. He declared in the message that Mexican troops had crossed the boundary of the United States, had invaded American territory, and had shed American blood on American soil. He ended the message with the words "War exists, and, notwithstanding all our efforts to avoid it, exists by the act of Mexico herself." He asked Congress to fulfill a requirement of the Constitution by formally declaring a war that was in progress. This was the first instance in American history when a president informed Congress of the existence of a war before a declaration of war had been made by Congress.

The boundary crossed by the Mexican force was the Rio Grande River. If the Rio Grande was truly the boundary, it had only recently become so, as recently as December 1845 when Texas was formally annexed to the Union by act of Congress. The alleged invasion occurred five and a half months after the annexation.

The Rio Grande had not been the boundary of Texas in earlier history. In 1816 the boundary had been set by the Spanish government at the Nueces River, which lies 130 miles north and east of the Rio Grande. The Nueces appeared on all reliable maps and atlases of the period as the boundary and had been accepted as such by many sturdy Americans, among them Stephen F. Austin, Andrew Jackson, Thomas Hart Benton, Martin Van Buren, and John C. Calhoun.

But in 1836, after Texas declared her independence and her army under Sam Houston won the smashing victory of San Jacinto, she claimed the Rio Grande as her line. In the battle, Santa Anna, the President of Mexico, was captured. In order to obtain release he signed, as a prisoner of war, an agreement that in a treaty later to be made, Texas might be permitted to extend as far as the Rio Grande. That agreement was repudiated at once by the Mexican Congress, which, under the Mexican Constitution, was the sole treaty-making body of the government. But Polk considered the agreement a treaty, and before Texas was formally admitted, he undertook to make the Rio Grande the boundary.

Another issue dividing the two governments was the damage claims of American citizens against Mexico. These had been advanced by persons who had suffered losses in Mexico in the course of the recurring Mexican revolutions. A mixed commission in 1840 had heard the claims, amounting to $8,500,000. It had found that the valid ones amounted to about a quarter of this sum. The rest were found fraudulent or heavily padded. The Mexican government agreed to pay the valid claims in installments, but after three had been paid it went bankrupt and defaulted on the remainder. The defaulted payments seemed to Polk a major American grievance. The total was afterward set by the American government at $3,250,000, not an enormous sum. American states and corporations were in default at this time on bonds in British possession to a total estimated at $200,000,000, as critics of the war pointed out.[1]

Another grievance of the Polk government was that Mexico refused to receive an American minister, John C. Slidell,

1. *Boston Whig* (daily), Dec. 23, 1846.

to settle these issues. Slidell had been sent by Polk in great secrecy to Mexico City in November 1845. He carried instructions that leaked out to the press—instructions to combine the issue of the unpaid damage claims with the issue of Mexican recognition of the Rio Grande boundary and, in addition, the sale of California and New Mexico to the United States. The Mexican government did not dare to receive Slidell, because it feared a revolt by an army under a military chieftain which lay outside the capital. It based its refusal on the ground that it had agreed only to discuss the issue of the annexation of Texas.

When news of the refusal reached Washington, Polk ordered the army of General Zachary Taylor to march to the Rio Grande. On reaching the river Taylor planted his cannon so as to command Matamoras, on the other side, and blockaded the river. This kept the Mexican army from receiving supplies by sea. The commander of the Mexican army sent a cavalry force across the river above Taylor's camp. This intercepted and surrounded a reconnoitering party of Taylor's, which tried to fight its way out. Several Americans were killed and the rest were taken prisoner. That was the American blood shed on American soil.

Accompanying Polk's special message came a bill to the House of Representatives drawn up by the Military Affairs Committee over the Sabbath. This authorized the President to accept militia and volunteers for military duty. The bill did not actually declare war. But a preamble was added to it on the floor by a Democratic war hawk, Representative William H. Brockenbough of Florida, which was said to be needed to give formal recognition to a state of war. In final form it read: "Whereas, by the act of . . . Mexico, a state of war exists between that government and the United States," the President is authorized to employ the militia and military forces to bring the war to a successful conclusion.[2]

That preamble, like the President's message, was greeted with instant denunciation. It was declared to be so bold a falsehood as to defile at the outset the whole bill. It was said to have been framed to commit everyone voting for the bill to the President's position that the war was defensive when patently it was aggressive—forced on Mexico by Polk. This initial reaction, immediately echoed by the Whig press, became the platform of the opposition during the remainder of the war.

Debate on the war bill was limited, by order of the majority, to two hours. Whig members asked for time to read the documents sent with the message. This was denied, though selected parts were read by the Clerk of the House. Protestors who rose to speak were not seen by the Speaker. Two of them succeeded in getting recognized by resorting to a parliamentary trick. They demanded permission to explain why they wanted to be excused from voting—a right that could not be denied. Both explained before they were cut off that the preamble was an utter falsehood.

Administration spokesmen upheld the stifling of debate on the ground of need to promptly rescue Taylor's army. The army was outnumbered and might be destroyed. The answer of the Whigs was that "Old Rough and Ready" was more than able to take care of himself, especially since he would be aided by militia from neighboring states. They also pointed out that, if Taylor was really in peril, aid from Washington could not reach him on time.

2. *Cong. Globe,* 29 Cong., 1 Sess., 792–795 (May 11, 1846). See also Frederick Merk, *Manifest Destiny and Mission in American History* (New York, Knopf, 1963), 89–91.

The war bill was passed two hours after it was received—by a vote that was overwhelming, 174 to 14. This was a victory for stampede tactics. The negative votes were nearly all from New England and from centers of New England influence in the West. At the head of the dissenters was John Quincy Adams. Five of the dissenters came from Massachusetts. Five more came from Ohio.

The Senate acted on the bill the next day. The tactics of stampede were there repeated. One day only was allowed for debate. Minority Senators protested, particularly at the denial of an opportunity to study the documents before voting. They thought the ordering of Taylor to the Rio Grande and his blocking off the river was as much an aggression as pointing a pistol at a man's breast. All the Whig speakers urged striking from the war bill the false and offensive preamble. Among the protestors a Southern Democrat—John C. Calhoun—was especially vehement. He said he would find it more impossible to vote that preamble than to plunge a dagger into his own heart. He went beyond the question who had been the aggressor, though he clearly thought Polk had been. He raised the more basic issue whether a local skirmish between parts of armies on the Rio Grande constituted war. War, he declared, required a declaration by Congress in both republics and he would not make war on Mexico by making war on *our* Constitution.[3]

The Senate's vote on the war bill was as lopsided as that of the House. It was 40 to 2. The courageous nays were both Whigs—John Davis of Massachusetts and John M. Clayton of Delaware. A number of Whigs voted "aye except the preamble." Calhoun refused to vote. Daniel Webster was absent.

3. *Cong. Globe*, 29 Cong., 1 Sess., 795–804 (May 12, 1846).

Calhoun said later that not 10 percent of Congress would have voted for the war bill if time had been given to examine the documents.

In the Boston press the same criticism was made of the war bill as had been made in Congress. The *Boston Whig*, an anti-slavery paper, which Charles Francis Adams and John G. Palfrey were soon to acquire, contained a letter from Charles Francis Adams in which he pronounced the preamble "one of the grossest national lies that was ever deliberately told."[4] He singled out for special attack Robert C. Winthrop, Boston's representative in Congress, who had voted for the war bill. He wrote that Winthrop by his vote had signed his name to a "national lie." Charles Sumner assailed Winthrop in the press with even greater bitterness. He wrote that Winthrop's hands were covered with blood, and by this language he broke up an old friendship. Palfrey, a notable clergyman and historian, was equally wrathful. These protestors all held that Polk was the aggressor and that his aggression was for the purpose of expansion over a helpless neighbor.

In the *New York Tribune* Horace Greeley expressed the same dissent. He wrote in an editorial sarcastically: "Grant the Father of Lies his premises, and he will prove himself a truth-teller and a saint by faultless logic. Shut your eyes to the whole course of events through the last twelve years . . . and it will become easy to prove that we are a meek, unoffending, ill used people, and that Mexico has kicked, cuffed and grossly imposed upon us. Only assume premises enough, as Polk does, and you may prove that it is New Or-

4. *Boston Whig* (d), June 2, 1846.

leans which has just been threatened with a cannonade instead of Matamoras, and that it is the Mississippi which has been formally blockaded by a stranger fleet and army instead of the Rio del Norte [Rio Grande].''[5]

In Washington the *National Intelligencer*, another of the nation's great Whig dailies, used similar language.

After the initial excitement at the war's opening the political parties of the country settled down to positions that became fixed. The Whigs, North and South, were highly critical of the war. The administration Democrats supported the war. In both parties, however, there were variations of criticism and of support.

The Northern Whigs became divided into conservatives and radicals. The conservatives emphasized the fraud and the aggressiveness of the war. They wished to avoid the added charge, made by the radicals, that the primary aim of the administration was the extension of slavery. Such a charge offended Southern Whigs, who, though opposed to the war, were slaveholders and were sensitive about attacks on slavery. Moreover, conservative Northern Whigs were not wholly persuaded that slavery extension *was* a primary aim of the administration.

In Massachusetts, Whigs upholding the moderate view included such politicians as Webster and Winthrop and such wealthy businessmen as Abbott Lawrence and Nathan Appleton, who were connected with the cotton belt by business ties. They were known as the Cotton Whigs. In Boston and in the North as a whole the conservatives outnumbered the radicals.

5. *New York Tribune* (d), May 13, 1846.

What were the facts which supported the conservative view that the war was not primarily for the extention of slavery? One fact, already mentioned, is that the Southern Whig leaders (slaveholders in every case) strenuously opposed the war. Henry Clay and John J. Crittenden, both from Kentucky, Alexander H. Stephens, George M. Berrien, Robert A. Toombs, all of Georgia, and many others, took that stand. Northern conservative Whigs, eager to retain this support, were fearful that if, in opposing the war, they added an antislavery stand to the anti-aggression stand, the unity of the party would be imperiled, and probably even the Union in the end. They recognized another obvious fact, militating against the radical explanation of the war, namely that many of the most rabid of the war hawks in the country were Northerners.

But radical Whigs were sure that the extension of slavery was a primary objective of the war. They were sure the ambition of the administration was to spread slavery over all Mexico and Central America. In Massachusetts those of such convictions included John Quincy Adams, Charles Francis Adams, Charles Sumner, Henry Wilson, and John G. Palfrey. These men and their followers were the Conscience Whigs—Whigs with a conscience not only regarding the iniquity of the aggression but the iniquity of its purpose—the spread of slavery.[6]

The Democrats were also divided. They had come into power as a result of victory in the presidential campaign of 1844, in which the platform had emphasized expansionism

6. Martin B. Duberman, *Charles Francis Adams* (Boston, Houghton Mifflin, 1961), chs. 12, 13; Frank O. Gatell, *John Gorham Palfrey* (Cambridge, Harvard University Press, 1963), chs. 9, 10.

—the immediate annexation of Texas and reoccupation of Oregon. That platform was a reflection of a belief recently come into prominence—the belief that it was the Manifest Destiny of the United States to expand over the entire continent of North America, from "the arctic to the tropic," as the slogan ran. I have dealt with that subject elsewhere and I do not intend to repeat it here except to say that during the Mexican War the belief in Manifest Destiny became focused on a demand to absorb All Mexico.

The conspicuous expansionists and war hawks were the administration Democrats—George Bancroft, Caleb Cushing, Lewis Cass, James Buchanan, Vice-president George M. Dallas, and Stephen A. Douglas. All were believers in Manifest Destiny. They had no very strong objections to slavery extension. They were willing to postpone the solution of the slavery problem to some future day. Their immediate ambition was territory. They were described contemptuously by the anti- slavery radicals as "doughfaces." At least two of the doughfaces were honored members of the Massachusetts Historical Society—George Bancroft as a resident member and Lewis Cass as a corresponding member.

But the Democratic party included others. It embraced a large minority of anti-slavery radicals, personified by John P. Hale of New Hampshire, David Wilmot of Pennsylvania, and Preston King of New York. It also included old-fashioned Jeffersonians, personified by an elder statesman of the party, Albert Gallatin. And, finally, it included Calhoun Democrats.

In view of all this diversity in both parties, how does the historian explain the overwhelming vote by which Congress declared the war? The explanation is found in a momentary hysteria on the part of the public which Polk converted into a stampede. Horace Greeley in an editorial explained the vote as a normal public response to an attack on the flag. The editorial was entitled "Our Country, Right or Wrong!" It ran:

"This is the spirit in which a portion of the Press, which admits that our treatment of Mexico has been ruffianly and piratical, and that the invasion of her territory by Gen. Taylor is a flagrant outrage, now exhorts our People to rally in all their strength, to lavish their blood and treasure in the vindictive prosecution of War on Mexico. We protest against such counsel. . . .

"We can easily defeat the armies of Mexico, slaughter them by thousands, and pursue them perhaps to their capital; we can conquer and 'annex' their territory; but what then? Have the histories of the ruin of Greek and Roman liberty consequent on such extensions of empire by the sword no lesson for us? Who believes that a score of victories over Mexico, the 'annexation' of half her provinces, will give us more Liberty, a purer Morality, a more prosperous Industry, than we now have? . . . Is not Life miserable enough, comes not Death soon enough, without resort to the hideous enginery of War?

"People of the United States! Your Rulers are precipitating you into a fathomless abyss of crime and calamity! Why sleep you thoughtless on its verge, as though this was not your business, or Murder could be hid from the sight of God by a few flimsy rags called banners? Awake and arrest the work of butchery ere it shall be too late to preserve your souls from the guilt of wholesale slaughter!"[7]

7. *New York Tribune* (d), May 12, 1846.

This editorial contained hard truth. An attack on the flag had been used by Polk to stampede the country into war. Such tactics were precisely what the framers of the Constitution had sought to prevent. They had sought to do it by writing the principle of checks and balances into the war provisions of the Constitution. A war-minded president was to be controlled by vesting in Congress the power to declare war and the power to provide supplies. The framers had faith in Congress because Congress represented diverse interests and because its minorities would keep a rein on majorities. All those precautions of the framers failed in the crisis of May 11 and 12, 1846. They failed because Polk had stampeded Congress and because minorities had failed to function.

The minorities failed in both parties. The Whigs did not function because they feared that if they voted against the war declaration they would meet the fate which had overtaken their predecessors, the Federalists, who had destroyed themselves by opposition in the War of 1812. Hesitant Democrats were equally quiet because their leaders had sponsored the joint resolution annexing Texas, a resolution which, by reason of its vague boundary provision, had produced the war.

Once the war declaration was approved by Whigs the party was committed to further support of the war. Most Whigs regularly voted supplies and men for the fighting, though they still denounced the war as iniquitous and unconstitutional. Even John Quincy Adams did this. Toward the end of 1847 he wrote Albert Gallatin, who was a fellow objector to the war: "The most remarkable circumstance of these transactions is that the war thus [unconstitutionally] made has been sanctioned by an overwhelming majority of both Houses . . . and is now sustained by similar majorities professing to disapprove its existence and pronouncing it unnecessary and unjust."[8] Abraham Lincoln, who entered Congress in 1847 and registered his protest against the war, regularly voted supplies for it.

The defense for voting supplies was set forth in the House by such Whigs as Winthrop, and, in the Senate, by John J. Crittenden. Congress, they pointed out, cannot abandon armies it has called into the field. Soldiers at the front cannot question orders on moral grounds. To do so would be subversive of all discipline. A war, right or wrong, which Congress has voted must be upheld.

In the House a radical anti-slavery Whig, Joshua R. Giddings from the Western Reserve of Ohio, challenged the worth of that reasoning. He cited the great British Whigs of the era of the American Revolution who announced in Parliament in 1776 their refusal to vote supplies for an unjust and oppressive war against America. Giddings proposed that similar means be used by American Whigs to force Polk out of Mexico. But Winthrop frowned on this revolutionary procedure and thought British precedent inapplicable in any case, for whereas in England the defeat of a supply measure brought down an administration and forced the creation of a new one, in the United States it would merely paralyze an administration which would still hang on.[9]

As the war progressed the conservative Whigs made fur-

8. J. Q. Adams to Albert Gallatin, Dec. 26, 1847, Adams Family Papers, Mass. Hist. Soc.

9. *Cong. Globe*, 29 Cong., 2 Sess., 143 ff. (Jan. 8, 1847), and Appendix, 47 ff. (Dec. 15, 1846).

ther adjustments of expediency to its demands. While always denouncing Polk they not only voted the supplies and men but lauded the gallantry of the front-line troops and the achievements of the generals leading them, especially the glory-covered Whig generals. On a number of occasions they voted resolutions of thanks to Generals Zachary Taylor and Winfield Scott.

These tactics were excellent politics and they paid high dividends. In the congressional election of 1846, which came half a year after the war declaration, the Whig party reversed the Democratic control of the House. The party acquired, in the next session of Congress, the control of the purse.

The loss of control of Congress in the midst of a highly successful war was to the Polk administration an unusual and humiliating experience. It was a clear measure of the moral protest which had developed against the war. What was equally significant was that the Whigs gained strength in all sections of the nation except in the interior of the South, and even there they stayed even.

The President sent his annual message to Congress soon after this rebuke. It was the message of December 8, 1846. In it he took a defensive stand. He devoted two thirds of the message to an elaboration of his earlier argument as to the origins of the war. He insisted that the boundary really was the Rio Grande and that the Mexican force, in crossing it, had invaded American soil and shed American blood there. He deplored Whig charges that *he* had been the aggressor. He thought those who made such charges were giving "aid and comfort to the enemy," which was saying that they were traitors.[10]

10. James D. Richardson (comp.): *Messages and Papers*, IV, 532 ff.

The message was greeted by a new explosion of wrath on the part of the Whigs. In Congress a Whig from the President's own state called the message "an artful perversion of the truth . . . to make the people believe a lie." The challenge of "lie" was thrown at the President again and again in Congress and in the press. The President's assurance that the Whig opposition was giving aid and comfort to the enemy was denounced as a "foul imputation" for purposes of intimidation, which would have the opposite effect of the one intended.[11]

In New England the President's review of the war's origins was met with biting sarcasm. An example is an editorial in the *Boston Whig*, written by Charles Francis Adams. It was addressed especially to the President's assertion that the war was supported by the great body of the American people. Adams observed:

"It is somewhat uncommon for a president who feels very sure that he is right, and also that the justice of his policy is understood by 'the great body of the people' to devote 2/3 of an annual message . . . to an effort to remove the scruples of a small minority of dissentients. It betrays a fatherly care of the stray sheep in his flock . . . [Moreover] the President does not . . . in December rest his justification of the war *solely* upon the ground selected by himself in May. That 'American blood should have been shed on American soil' was deemed in the spring ample cause for the call . . . to arms. It is now held not quite defense enough . . . without bringing in a long array of old offenses committed by Mexico."[12]

11. *Cong. Globe*, 29 Cong., 2 Sess., Appendix, 56 ff. (Dec. 16, 1846).
12. *Boston Whig* (d), Dec. 18, 1846.

In April 1847 the Massachusetts legislature adopted a set of resolutions still more condemnatory. The resolutions lifted the slavery issue into prominence. They read:

"Resolved that the present war with Mexico . . . was unconstitutionally commenced by the order of the President to General Taylor to take military possession of territory in dispute . . . and that it is now waged by a powerful nation against a weak neighbor . . . at immense cost of treasure and life, for the dismemberment of Mexico, and for the conquest of . . . territory from which slavery has been . . . excluded, with the triple object of extending slavery, of strengthening the slave power, and of obtaining the control of the Free States. . . . That such a war of conquest, so hateful in its objects, so wanton, unjust and unconstitutional in its origin and character, must be regarded as a war against freedom, against humanity, against justice, against the Union, . . . and against the free states. . . ."[13]

These resolutions were approved by overwhelming majorities in both houses. They were based to a large extent on a report Charles Sumner had written for a committee of the legislature. In the report Sumner had taken the radical stand that Congress should withhold supplies from the armed forces.[14] But the state legislature refused to go that far.

The growing bitterness of the radicals against the war appeared in a startling speech delivered in the United States Senate on February 11, 1847, by Thomas Corwin, a Whig of Ohio. He denounced the war as "flagrant," "a usurpa-

13. *Massachusetts Acts and Resolves, 1847*, ch. 103 (April 26, 1847).

14. *Massachusetts House Documents*, 1847, no. 187, pp. 1–35. Sumner's Report, including his proposal to withhold supplies, is reprinted in *Old South Leaflets*, VI, no. 132.

tion of authority," "a senseless quest for more room," a quest he would, if he were a Mexican, respond to with the words: "Have you not room in your own country to bury your dead men? If you come into mine we will greet you with bloody hands and welcome you to hospitable graves." He predicted that the war would generate a sectional clash over slavery and plunge the sister states of the Union into the bottomless gulf of civil conflict.[15] The speech seemed traitorous to conservative Whigs and to conservative Democrats. But to such radical Whigs as Charles Francis Adams and Joshua Giddings it seemed admirable. They thought hopefully of Corwin as a candidate in 1848 for the presidency.[16]

In December 1847 the Congress chosen the preceding year convened in Washington and took the necessary measures to organize itself. One step was the election of a Whig speaker of the House. A contest developed in this process between the conservative Whigs and the Conscience Whigs, which brought to the surface all the bitterness that had developed between them. Robert C. Winthrop was the leading conservative candidate, but on the first ballot he was short three votes of a House majority necessary for election. The three holdouts were Palfrey, Giddings, and Amos Tuck of New Hampshire, all of them radical anti-slavery men. They held out because Winthrop had shown half-heartedness in opposing the war and because, as speaker, he would appoint committees that would support war measures. In the end he won the speakership, but only after several conservative Whigs, who had been voting for other candidates, switched to him

15. *Cong. Globe,* 29 Cong., 2 Sess., Appendix, 217 (Feb. 11, 1847).
16. C. F. Adams to J. R. Giddings, Feb. 22, 1847. Adams Family Papers, Mass. Hist. Soc.

and canceled his deficit of votes.[17] One of the Whigs who voted for him from the beginning was John Quincy Adams. He voted so because of an old friendship with Winthrop's father. Afterwards there was an embarrassing situation between the younger Adams and the elder, because the elder had abandoned his principles.

While the anti-war feeling in the North was intensifying, the armies of the United States were battering down Mexican resistance. One army under Taylor held the north; the other, under Scott, moved toward Mexico City from Vera Cruz. Both armies were winning spectacular victories against great odds.

The appetite of the All Mexico men was thus stimulated. The All Mexico movement and the related Manifest Destiny movement reached a climax during the second half of the war. Those ideas were especially attractive to the great urban masses of the northeastern seaboard: the city Democrats, in considerable part immigrants, the "unterrified Democracy" of New York City and Tammany Hall. The penny press of New York fed these ideas to its readers. So did the penny press of Philadelphia, Baltimore, and Boston. In Boston, the *Boston Times* was the great expansionist teacher. In the interior, Illinois was an outstanding center of All Mexico feeling.[18]

The South was hesitant about accepting the program of All Mexico. Absorption would mean extending citizenship to colored and mixed races. Extending citizenship to colored and mixed races ran counter to all Southern instincts. It

17. *Cong. Globe*, 30 Cong., 1 Sess., pp. 2, 3 (Dec. 6, 1847).
18. Merk, *Manifest Destiny and Mission*, chs. 5 and 6.

clashed especially with the instincts of Calhoun, who was the voice of Southern racism. His speeches in Congress were a bitter assault on the All Mexico movement on this ground. He felt that if any Mexican territory were to be taken, it should be only the sparsely populated northern parts—California and New Mexico. Even these areas he hesitated to accept because he doubted they were suitable for slavery. He wanted no territory that would spawn free states.

The great military successes in Mexico were most frightening to the radicals. They seemed to open a growing opportunity for slavery expansion. That foreboding had been reflected early in the war in a rider attached to a bill desired by Polk for two million dollars with which to negotiate a peace with Mexico. The rider was the famous Wilmot proviso of August 1846, declaring that none of the territory acquired from Mexico should ever be open to slavery or involuntary servitude. This represented an evolution from mere protest to an attempt to restrict the administration. It created tremendous excitement in Congress and in the country. It failed on the last day of the session but was attached again and again to war bills thereafter. It was never adopted. It was defeated always by a Southern opposition that was unanimous, aided by the votes of Northern "doughfaces."

The Wilmot proviso was the most ominous of the protests generated by the war. It was ominous because it so sharply divided the nation into quarreling sections. It did just what conservative Whigs had feared the most. Its support in Congress was exclusively Northern. Outside of Congress ten Northern state legislatures, by resolutions in one form or another, voted for it. It represented a Northern coalition of anti-slavery radicals. It was what Thomas Corwin had proph-

6. This anti-war cartoon, appearing eight and a half months before the Treaty of Guadalupe Hidalgo, recognized the aims of the Polk administration and was a forecast of the result of the war. From *Yankee Doodle*, a humorous New York weekly, May 15, 1847.

esied in his radical speech. It led Calhoun to despair of the Union.

What was the answer given by Whig conservatives to the growing Wilmotism of the North? It was as simple as the omission of one word from the Wilmot prescription of "No more slave territory." The new prescription was "No more territory." The omission of the word "slave" was designed to quiet the disruptive moral overtones of the Wilmot proviso, and to draw the sting that offended the Southern slaveholding society. "No more territory" was neutral on slavery and held Northern and Southern Whigs together. It spurned as immoral only the Polk program of brutal territorial conquest. For just this reason it was not enough for Northern moralists. These distinctions were explained with care by Horace Greeley in his editorials.[19]

Some conservative Whigs and even some radicals were willing to compromise, however, about taking territory if it was territory that would not support slavery. Also they insisted that the territory be obtained only in exchange for our assuming the claims of American citizens or by purchase from Mexico. Whigs were attracted especially by Upper California with its magnificent harbor of San Francisco. Northern commercial Whigs would particularly have liked to obtain part or all of Upper California. Webster considered the port of San Francisco alone to be twenty times as valuable as the whole of Texas.

While these party responses to the war were being made, Scott's army irresistibly pounded its way to the heart of Mexico. By the early autumn of 1847 it had taken Mexico City by storm and the American flag flew over the Halls of the

19. *New York Tribune* (d), Sept. 8, 1847.

Montezumas. That thrilled expansionists and opened the prospect of obtaining the kind of peace they wanted.

Before discussing the efforts at peace, I should like to put aside politics for a moment and refer to dissent in American literary circles. Ralph Waldo Emerson was disgusted with the war, predicting that the United States would absorb Mexico "as the man swallows the arsenic, which brings him down in turn."[20] But he was too engrossed in his own pursuits to actively enter the anti-war ranks. His friend, Henry Thoreau, became an activist when he delivered his famous lecture in which he urged "The Duty of Civil Disobedience" against any government that condoned slavery and engaged in unjust war. James Russell Lowell denounced the war and Manifest Destiny in his satirical *Biglow Papers.* William Ellery Channing, the poet, condemned the war in verse in the Whig press. Samuel Gridley Howe, Theodore Parker, and Wendell Phillips eloquently denounced the war.

In the Massachusetts Historical Society diversity regarding the war was the rule. Here were the bitter anti-slavery radicals, the two Adamses and Palfrey. Here also were the conservatives, Daniel Webster, Robert C. Winthrop, Edward Everett, and Nathan Appleton. Here was George Bancroft, of Polk's cabinet, and finally here was the arch expansionist, Lewis Cass.

This diversity of opinion could have livened the meetings of the Society—especially if such a topic as "Dissent in Three Wars" had been approved by the program committee. But no such program was ever considered. While the world outside was torn asunder and members of the Society almost slugged each other on the streets, each meeting was as placid

20. *Journals of Ralph Waldo Emerson* (E. W. Emerson and W. E. Forbes, eds., Boston, 1912), VII, 206.

as an oyster in a shell. And this placidity was excellent for the Society, as witness the magnificent gifts to the Society of the great collections of member correspondence, which have made its holdings among the richest in the world for the period of the Mexican War.

As for the efforts at peace, they were pressed by Polk even in an early stage of the fighting. He had learned indirectly from Santa Anna, who was then in Cuba as an exile wanting to get back home, that if he were allowed as a former leader to return, he would overthrow the Mexican government and would negotiate a treaty of peace with the United States that would include a cession of territory. This prospect attracted Polk, and orders were given the American navy to let Santa Anna slip through the blockade. Santa Anna did slip through, and he did effect a successful overthrow of the Mexican government. But instead of entering into peace negotiations he reorganized the Mexican resistance; and the only result of the maneuver was more strenuous fighting for the rest of the war.

That story was made known to Congress and to the press late in 1846 by the opposition Whigs. Polk's tactics were described as contemptible for a great state to use in fighting a weak one. A Southern Whig summed up the sentiments of many others in Congress. He did it in the form of rhetorical questions: "Does history furnish an example of more abhorrent perfidy? Was any government through its chief magistrate ever more vilely prostituted?"[21]

21. These questions were raised by Garrett Davis of Kentucky in Congress on December 22, 1846, in revealing the Santa Anna intrigue. George Ashmun, of Massachusetts, who had voted against the declaration of war, retold the story early in 1847, and proposed a resolution of inquiry to the President concerning it, which the Democratic majority voted down. *Cong. Globe*, 29 Cong., 2 Sess., 297–298 (Jan. 30, 1847); and *ibid.*, Appendix, 104 ff. (Dec. 22, 1846).

TRIUMPH OF THE LETHEON.

7. Cartoon from *Yankee Doodle* of April 10, 1847, shows the one-legged Mexican president, Santa Anna, losing his other leg, labeled "New Mexico." The flask of $3,000,000 represents the Act of March 3, 1847, "to enable the President to conclude a treaty of peace." Letheon is an old trade name for ether as an anesthetic, first used for an amputation at the Massachusetts General Hospital in the autumn of 1846. President James K. Polk administers the $3,000,000 anesthetic while Senator Thomas Hart Benton wields the saw.

Polk continued for another year his efforts to bring Santa Anna into peace negotiations. He entrusted negotiations to Nicholas P. Trist, Chief Clerk of the State Department. Trist operated under the wing of Scott's army while it was advancing on Mexico City. Late in August 1847 an armistice was arranged and a Mexican peace offer was obtained, which was not, however, very genuine. The Mexicans proposed among other things that a buffer state—a kind of neutral zone—be erected in the disputed area between the Nueces and the Rio Grande. This was a throwback to the old boundary dispute. Trist rejected it, but was incautious enough to send it, with the other proposals, for reference to his government. Polk was infuriated with his agent for showing weakness regarding the sensitive issue of the origins of the war. He canceled Trist's powers, rebuked him, and ordered him home. These orders were late in arriving. By the time they reached Trist, Mexico City had been captured, Santa Anna was in disgrace, and the new government was ready to negotiate in earnest. With this government Trist, in defiance of his orders, but supported by Scott, negotiated the treaty of Guadalupe Hidalgo of February 2, 1848. The treaty took from Mexico more than a third of her territory. Yet it was the most lenient treaty Trist could sign under Polk's instructions.

Trist reckoned that the President would be compelled to accept the treaty in spite of its irregular negotiation. And he was right. For the nation was utterly weary of the war, was suspicious of the ever-promised peace that like a mirage was never reached, and was dangerously divided over the issue of the extension of slavery. The House of Representatives was controlled by the peace party. If the President were to

8. A dividing line at the Isthmus of Tehuantepec is proposed to the dismay of the Mexican onlookers. The cartoon, which is from *Yankee Doodle* of August 28, 1847, misrepresents the personal views of Polk's negotiator, Nicholas P. Trist.

AN AVAILABLE CANDIDATE.
THE ONE QUALIFICATION FOR A WHIG PRESIDENT.

9 and 10. President Polk had ruled himself out of the presidential race of 1848. General Zachary Taylor, the war hero, emerged as the strongest man for the Whigs and Senator Lewis Cass of Michigan for the Democrats. Both candidates were bitterly attacked for their association with the Mexican War. At the left is a print circulated during the election year, depicting General Taylor as "an available candidate" seated in triumph atop a mound of skulls. The cartoon above, another print circulated in 1848, shows Senator Cass, whom Polk privately favored for the Democratic nomination, waving a "Manifest Destiny" sword and calling not only for Mexico but also for Cuba and Peru. Deemed a bag of wind by the Whigs, he is represented as a cannon belching "gas"—a play on words.

spurn the treaty giving the United States the sparsely populated northern part of Mexico, the Whigs would declare this to be proof of their charge that the war had been begun to seize All Mexico. The House might refuse further supplies, in which case even California and New Mexico might be lost. Dissenters such as Gallatin and Calhoun were deploring the fiscal burdens of the war. The press was charging that while the war was draining the nation's resources, urgent domestic needs were not being met.[22] Polk decided, therefore, to submit the treaty to the Senate, where it was promptly ratified, with alterations not affecting the boundary provisions. The vote to ratify was 38 to 14.[23]

This big affirmative vote reflected a universal demand for peace. Even Horace Greeley desired ratification in order to end the slaughter in Mexico.[24] The big vote reflected also a wide tolerance for acquisitions which were thought unsuitable for slavery.

The fourteen negative votes reflected dissatisfaction with the treaty on diverse grounds. Six were from expansionists who felt defrauded because the treaty did not take enough.

22. *New York Tribune* (d), Feb. 5, 1848. The *Tribune* listed internal improvements among the neglected needs.

23. *Sen. Exec. Docs.*, 30 Cong., 1 Sess. (Serial 509), no. 52.

24. Rumors of the treaty's content arrived in advance of it. An editorial in the *New York Tribune* (d) of January 27, 1848, concluded as follows: "As to the presumed Treaty, we hope the Senate will ratify anything Mr. Polk may send them, even in the sneaking, underhand fashion of his Oregon Treaty. Peace! Peace! even though we pay Fifteen Millions of Dollars for it and take a thousand miles of inhospitable deserts haunted by implacably hostile savages as a consideration, in order that Polk & Co. may boast of their conquests and annexations. Sign anything, ratify anything, pay anything, to end the guilt, the bloodshed, the shame, the enormous waste of this horrible contest. Even with that most unfit, unstable boundary of the Rio Grande, give us Peace; and then for the reckoning!"

Seven were from Whigs who thought the treaty took too much. Thomas Hart Benton, a Democrat, voted nay, probably because he felt as the Whigs did.

A question arises in conclusion. How effective was dissent in the war? The question necessitates asking another. What would the treaty have been except for the dissent? The answer is that it would have been even harsher. Much more of Mexico would have been taken. Dissent moderated the treaty by revealing the dangers of the programs of All Mexico and Manifest Destiny.

On the other hand, the war and the dissent left behind sectional strains that began the process of breaking the old bonds of union, especially the national political parties, and replacing them with sectionalized parties. In the fierce struggles occurring over the organization of the Mexican cession, the Free Soil party was born, the crisis of 1850 occurred, and the Republican party was foreshadowed, which, when it triumphed in 1860, led to the secession of the Southern states. These effects illustrate an old truth: that moral issues are not easily quieted when they are as basic as those raised by Polk in 1846. They remain in the earth like dragon's teeth to grow into future armed conflict.

3

Frank Freidel

Dissent in the Spanish-American War and the Philippine Insurrection

The tragic irony of the Spanish-American War and its aftermath is one of the best-known themes of modern American history. In 1898 the United States, for what seemed to be compelling humanitarian reasons, embarked upon a small war to liberate Cuban insurrectionaries from Spanish tyranny. A few months later, the United States emerged a colonial power, the possessors of the spoils of war, and drifted into lengthy and costly guerrilla warfare against insurrectionaries fighting for the independence of the Philippine Islands. The Spanish-American War, lasting only a hundred days, was too brief and too successful to become unpopular, but the cruel campaigns against the Filipino *insurrectos* brought forth vehement dissent. And, as during the War of 1812 and the Mexican War, a focal point of the protest was New England.[1]

Since the dissent was concentrated on a cruel jungle warfare aimed at denying a people their freedom, it carried much the same sort of indignant resentment which had

1. This paper is both impressionistic and focused upon New England. It owes much to the scholarly writing upon the imperialism and anti-imperialism of the turn of the century, especially to R. L. Beisner, *Twelve Against Empire: The Anti-Imperialists, 1898–1900* (New York, McGraw-Hill, 1968); F. H. Harrington, "The Anti-Imperialist Movement in the United States," *Mississippi Valley Historical Review*, 22 (1935), 211–230; E. R. May, *Imperial Democracy: The Emergence of America as a Great Power* (New York, Harcourt, Brace & World, 1961); May, *American Imperialism: A Speculative Essay* (New York, Atheneum, 1968); and H. W. Morgan, *America's Road to Empire: The War With Spain and Overseas Expansion* (New York, Wiley, 1965).

taken the nation into war against Spain to liberate Cuba. It also bore some resemblance to protests in the 1960's against the war in Vietnam. Indeed at some points the parallels are so close that by selecting certain factors, one could give the impression that history had repeated itself. Yet in other, fundamental respects, the anger of the early 1900's and the impasse of the 1960's were quite different, even in the protest against them. Many of these parallels, and these differences, become readily apparent as one examines the earlier events.

By the 1890's, the United States, like the great powers of Europe, had moved into the industrial age, and was beginning to obtain some of the new ambitions and the new weapons—at least a few new armored warships—which were a prelude to the escalating of war into world dimensions. As yet there was no thought of future horrors, but rather, among a newer generation which had grown up in this country during the peaceable decades since the close of the Civil War, an envy of the powers of Europe for the adventure that their young men could enjoy at little real danger, in the cause of empire, subduing savage peoples who were resisting the advance of civilization on some distant frontier. Among older men who had fought in the Civil War, a nostalgia for bygone glory had replaced the trauma of hardship, despair, and gore which, at the time, the war had meant for most of them. There was, among many people, regardless of age, a feeling that the United States was missing out in the rush for empire, that this nation too should seek markets for its industry, new sources of raw materials—at least of tropical products—and areas for investment. Old Glory should fly over palm as well as pine, where distant coaling stations could serve a powerful navy, controlling the sealanes of the world, and where backward peoples under benign tutelage would learn the mysteries of the superior Anglo-Saxon culture. In short, as the *Literary Digest* suggested in April 1895, Americans were spoiling for a war. Crisis followed crisis, until the right war—a small war—came along.

This spirit almost embroiled the nation in the wrong war—a conflict with Great Britain, which with its infinitely more powerful navy could have inflicted disaster upon the United States. Cool heads prevailed in the dispute that broke out with Britain in 1895 over, of all things, the boundary between Venezuela and British Guiana. But William James noted, "It is instructive to find how near the surface in all of us the old fighting spirit lies and how slight an appeal will wake it up. Once *really* waked, there is no retreat."[2] Some of the cooler heads during this crisis of 1895–1896 were to be found in Boston and Cambridge. Theodore Roosevelt wrote indignantly to the editors of the *Harvard Crimson* on January 2, 1896, complaining because various Harvard professors and students had opposed President Cleveland's ultimatum to England:

"The Stock-jobbing timidity, the Baboo kind of statesmanship, which is clamored for at this moment by the men who put monetary gain before national honor, or who are still intellectually in a state of colonial dependence on England, would in the end most assuredly invite war. . . . If Harvard men wish peace with honor they will heartily support the [government] in the Venezuela matter; will demand . . . the

2. William James to Frederic Myers, Jan. 1, 1896, cited in Barbara W. Tuchman, *The Proud Tower: A Portrait of the World before the War, 1890–1914* (New York, Macmillan, 1966), 139.

strictest application of the Monroe Doctrine; and will farther demand that immediate preparation be made to build a really first-class Navy."[3]

Several days later, Roosevelt complained to his bellicose friend, Senator Henry Cabot Lodge: "The *Harvard Graduates Magazine* is now assailing me with the ineffective bitterness proper to beings whose cult is nonvirility."[4]

It was T.R.'s sort of spirit, together with the almost irresistible demands of humanitarianism, that brought the United States into war against Spain little more than two years later. The feeling grew that the only way to rescue the Cuban people from misery and even death was through American intervention. This feeling disarmed many of the political, religious, and business leaders who customarily opposed foreign ventures, who had counseled caution during the Venezuelan crisis, and were to become bitter opponents of the annexation and subjugation of the Philippine Islands.

Even had these normal opponents of war not been neutralized, the Spanish-American War would have been hard to avoid. In recent years, historians have rejected earlier assumptions that yellow journalism, mass hysteria, and the inability of President McKinley to resist pressure brought an unjust American declaration of war after Spain had capitulated to our demands. There has also been a questioning of economic factors, although one recent writer, Walter LaFeber, still gives them emphasis.[5] The fact is that as early

3. Theodore Roosevelt to editors, *Harvard Crimson*, Jan. 2, 1896, in E. E. Morison, J. M. Blum, and J. J. Buckley, eds., *The Letters of Theodore Roosevelt* (8 vols., Cambridge, Mass., Harvard University Press, 1951–1954), I, 505–506.

4. Roosevelt to Henry Cabot Lodge, Jan. 19, 1896, *ibid.*, 509.

5. Walter LaFeber, *The New Empire: An Interpretation of American Expansion, 1860–1898* (Ithaca, Cornell University Press, 1963).

as the Grant administration there was the possibility that the United States might intervene in Cuba to put down the lengthy and stalemated conflict which broke out in 1868 between the Spanish authorities and the insurrectionaries.

After ten years that war ended in an unsatisfactory settlement, no more than a truce, and fresh conflict erupted in 1895. The authorities resumed an endless chase of ill-armed guerrillas who could control the countryside but could not capture the cities or obtain the support of their considerable Spanish populace. Young Winston Churchill, seeking excitement, came from England to write dispatches on the war for the New York *World*. His account of a minor skirmish was an accurate description of most of the fighting in Cuba—and later in the Philippines. He advanced with a small Spanish force across a clearing toward Cubans hidden in the underbrush: "The insurgents are bad shots. It appeared to me that tons of lead passed over the heads of General Valdez's staff, with whom I was. Three orderlies were wounded. . . . My general conclusion is that European methods of warfare are almost out of the question in a wild countryside."[6] A few days after this, Churchill was in New York. His sympathies later, when war came, were with the United States. There was never the faintest possibility that he would be atop San Juan Hill when Theodore Roosevelt came charging up.

Ineffectual though this sort of warfare was, it created chaos in Cuba. By 1898 large parts of the island had been desolated, and correspondents were sending highly exaggerated reports that a quarter of the population was dead

6. Winston Churchill, dispatch from Havana, Dec. 5, 1895, cited in C. H. Brown, *The Correspondents' War: Journalists in the Spanish-American War* (New York, Scribner's, 1967), 26.

already. Certainly hunger and disease were spreading—and yellow fever was advancing into the southern United States. It seemed intolerable to allow such conditions to continue only ninety miles from Key West, Florida.

President Cleveland, a conspicuous foe of imperialism, pressed Spain to introduce reforms in Cuba and warned of the possibility of American intervention. McKinley, coming into office in 1897, somewhat modified Cleveland's policies but continued the pressure on Spain. As Ernest May has pointed out after researching in Spanish archives, Spain did not, and could not, make significant concessions. McKinley, far from having "no more backbone than a chocolate eclair," as either—perhaps both—Speaker Thomas B. Reed or Theodore Roosevelt is supposed to have suggested, pursued a careful, deliberate course. There was a growing pressure upon Congress. The senior Senator from Massachusetts, George F. Hoar, complained, "Every congressman has two or three newspapers in his district, most of them printed in red ink, shouting for blood." After the battleship *Maine* unexplainably blew up in Havana harbor in February 1898, killing 260 of the crew, the shouts became hysterical. But it was not the slogan "Remember the Maine" that brought war. Rather, McKinley, firmly backed by Congress, felt that only through war against Spain could the endless sufferings of the Cubans be brought to an end.[7]

There was, nevertheless, sufficient opposition to war to make that enthusiastic jingoist, Roosevelt, the Assistant Secretary of the Navy, decidedly nervous. He complained only two weeks before the war declaration that the President was determined to have peace at any price (which was quite

7. May, *Imperial Democracy,* 160–177.

obviously untrue) but that Congress as a whole wanted war or action that would lead to it. Yet, wrote Roosevelt, "The most influential man in it, Tom Reed, is as much against war as the President, and the group of Senators who stand closest to the President [presumably Roosevelt meant Senator Hoar] are also ferociously against war. . . . Therefore I think it about a toss up whether we have war or peace."[8] Speaker of the House Reed was adamantly against war, and cutting in his derision toward the jingoes. When Senator Redfield Proctor of Vermont, an owner of marble quarries, spoke in favor of fighting Spain, Reed commented, "Proctor's position might have been expected. A war will make a large market for gravestones." There was no need for Roosevelt, the self-avowed advocate of what others called "jingo doctrines," to be nervous. Reed was almost alone in his flat opposition to a declaration of war. Senator Hoar, although expressing his hope that it could be avoided, was willing to bend to humanitarian (and perhaps party) considerations; he affirmed his readiness to support the President with all his heart if war came.[9]

Congress did declare war in April 1898, and only five days later there came the surprising and spectacular news that the Asiatic Squadron under Commodore George Dewey had destroyed the Spanish fleet in Manila Bay.

In the aftermath of Dewey's victory, to express publicly one's opposition to the war required rare hardihood. This, that benign old aristocrat, Professor Charles Eliot Norton,

8. Theodore Roosevelt to Douglas Robinson, March 30, 1898, *Letters of Theodore Roosevelt*, II, 805.

9. Tuchman, *Proud Tower*, 150. Roosevelt wrote in March 1898, "Now, I have consistently preached what our opponents are pleased to call 'jingo doctrines' for a good many years." *Letters of Theodore Roosevelt*, II, 803.

possessed in full measure. He urged Harvard students not to enlist in a war in which "we jettison all that was most precious of our national cargo." The war, he declared in June 1898, was "a turning-back from the path of civilization to that of barbarism." The effort to alleviate Cuban suffering would result in "inflicting worse suffering still." Senator Hoar lashed out at his old classmate: "The trouble with Professor Norton, who thinks his countrymen are lacking in a sense of honour, is that there are two things he cannot in the least comprehend—he cannot comprehend his countrymen, and he cannot comprehend honour."[10]

Though the Spanish-American War lasted too short a time, and was too filled with thrilling victories, to bring serious dissent, it was certainly not a "splendid little war" as John Hay so inappropriately said. It was a grueling ordeal for those who fought in it. They were rescued from the ineptitude and blunders of their superiors only by the more gross ineptitude and gallant defeatism of the Spanish forces. There had been nervous excitement along the Atlantic Coast during a lengthy period when Admiral Pascual Cervera's Spanish fleet was unaccounted for. The ships slipped past American forces into Santiago harbor in eastern Cuba, where the American fleet bottled them. The American strategy then was to send an expeditionary force to dislodge Spanish troops from fortifications ringing Santiago and to drive out the Spanish fleet. On May 26, General William R. Shafter received orders to depart from Tampa with his forces; June 14 came before 16,000 of them could set forth on a strange array of ships. It was an incredible flotilla of 32 transports and numerous accompanying vessels, lumbering at no more than seven

10. Beisner, *Twelve Against Empire*, 80, 150, 237.

miles an hour for five and a half days, much of the time within sight of the Cuban coast. At night the ships were clearly visible with their running lights, and the headquarters ship was brightly lit with a band on deck playing ragtime. But neither enroute, nor during the days then spent unloading at the base of a 230-foot nob topped by a Spanish blockhouse—not during this whole period—was a shot fired at them. A little later, the long day's battle to capture San Juan Hill and the other outlying fortifications around Santiago was bloody enough; it decimated the American force. Illness followed, but before it could become serious, Cervera's fleet sallied forth to its destruction, and the campaign in Cuba was at an end. Compared with the national jubilation, the recriminations and counter-recriminations concerning the less effective aspects of both the army and navy campaigns were relatively insignificant. In mid-August, Spain sued for peace, and the war was over.

Simultaneously, across the Pacific, the way had been prepared for a new and more serious struggle, the Philippine insurrection. It was to evoke lengthy and bitter dissent.

Though it was a humanitarian sentiment that carried the United States into the war to liberate Cuba, certain imperialists for some time had had their covetous eyes upon the Philippines. The naval coup in Manila Bay was the outgrowth of serious discussion and planning, at least since February 1898. It was not a sudden impulse that led to the dispatch of Dewey's fleet as soon as war was declared. Far more significant was the next step, which almost inevitably would lead to the annexation of at least some territory. President McKinley may indeed not have known within two thousand miles where the islands were, as he later remarked, but he did quickly make the momentous decision to order

American forces to the Philippines. This was an entirely unnecessary move if the defeat of Spain were his only object.

On the other hand, Dewey allowed the youthful Filipino rebel leader, General Emilio Aguinaldo, to return from exile. The Filipino forces gathered such strength that they soon brought Manila under siege and in the summer of 1898 assumed control of large parts of the islands before the arrival of the American troops. Aguinaldo on July 1 proclaimed himself President of the Philippine Republic, but cold instructions came from the Secretary of State in Washington that the United States in occupying the islands would "expect from the inhabitants . . . that obedience which will be lawfully due from them." If McKinley had not already decided upon annexation, neither was he ready to close the option, which was already gaining enthusiastic adherents. In mid-August after the American troops had arrived, a final farcical battle took place between the United States and Spain. The two sides planned it to be bloodless so that Spain could surrender the city to the Americans, who had promised to keep the Filipino *insurrectos* out. The battle was not quite bloodless, because insurgents became involved, but when it was over, the Americans possessed Manila and, on orders from the White House, firmly barred Aguinaldo's men from participating in a joint occupation. The Filipino patriots began at once turning the former Spanish fortifications outside Manila into offensive positions from which they might besiege the Americans in the city. Months of tense waiting followed until it could be seen what the disposition of the Philippines was to be.[11]

11. For popular accounts of the war, see Walter Millis, *The Martial Spirit* (New York, 1931), and Frank Freidel, *The Splendid Little War* (Boston, Little, Brown, 1958).

Within the United States during that summer of 1898, a vigorous struggle between imperialists and anti-imperialists began. Talk of empire, of a United States abandoning its hemispheric isolation and assuming a leading role in world politics, was a heady intoxicant that few could resist. Brooks Adams, cycling with Oliver Wendell Holmes, Jr., at Beverly Farms and expounding to him his expansionist ideas, won Holmes's admiration. "He thinks this war is the first gun in the battle for the ownership of the world," Holmes reported to a friend. "I confess to pleasure in hearing some rattling jingo talk after the self-righteous and preaching discourse, which has prevailed to some extent at Harvard College & elsewhere."[12] Brooks Adams' brother Henry, by complex reasoning, arrived at some interesting conclusions: "So we can foresee a new centralization, of which Russia is one pole, and we the other, with England between. The Anglo-American alliance is almost inevitable."[13]

The common man, as McKinley discovered when he took a junket around the Middle West delivering small ambivalent speeches as he went, found rather appealing the thought of the American flag, like the Union Jack, flying over exotic realms. There was also, in that quite racist era, a general willingness to regard smaller, brown-skinned people as inferiors, scarcely entitled to the privileges of self-government. Already, strong misgivings had arisen over Cuba, where the white troops had developed an antipathy for their Cuban allies, so often mulatto or black, and a corresponding readiness to fraternize with the defeated Spanish foe. The same informal caste lines developed in the Philippines, where the

12. A. F. Beringause, *Brooks Adams: A Biography* (New York, Knopf, 1955), 166.
13. *Ibid.*, 172–173.

Americans immediately became the successors to the Spanish overlords.

From the day of victory at Manila Bay onward, the anti-imperialists, insistent that the war not be turned into one of annexation, had raised their voices. They futilely opposed the annexation of the Hawaiian Islands and insisted that the United States must make good on its pledge of Cuban independence. Concerning the acquisition of Puerto Rico, interestingly enough, they had little to say, presumably because no protest seemed to be forthcoming from Puerto Ricans. Rather, the anti-imperialists concentrated their vehemence in fighting against the forcible acquisition of the Philippines. Their arguments were moral, humanitarian, economic, military, and racist—a wide array, ranging from a fear of America's vulnerability if it became involved in East Asian politics to an insistence that the nation must live up to the traditions of the Declaration of Independence. Their rallying cry was a quotation from President McKinley's message to Congress in December 1897 in which (concerning Cuba) he had declared, "I speak not of forcible annexation, for that cannot be thought of. That by our code of morality would be criminal aggression."

Yet it became amply clear late in 1898, when the United States obtained from an unwilling Spain a treaty ceding the Philippines in return for $20,000,000, that annexation would have to be forcible. It was almost certain to involve armed conflict with the Filipinos.

Opponents to the annexation of the Philippines organized themselves at Boston in November 1898 into the Anti-Imperialist League. Other leagues sprang up elsewhere, and a year later national headquarters opened in Chicago. The

Anti-Imperialists were an interesting combination of Republicans, Mugwumps, and Democrats. Some of the members had fought bitterly on differing sides of the political battles of the past generation. For the most part their leaders, as Robert Beisner and others have pointed out, were elderly respected reformers of Liberal Republican and Mugwump antecedents, looking to bygone traditions. On the other hand, the leading Democrat, William Jennings Bryan, was youthful and several of the most eloquent pamphleteers were men in their early thirties: to cite two, the Rev. Adolph A. Berle and Charles Warren.[14]

The anti-imperialists almost but not quite won the battle to defeat the treaty at least temporarily. To have done so would have accentuated divisions in the Republican party and been humiliating to McKinley, but would not have avoided the acquisition of colonies and a colonial war. The President could have called the new Congress into special session in March 1899 and obtained ratification from a Senate more heavily pro-administration in its membership. The fact that ultimate victory in any event was to come to the imperialists did little at the time to dull interest in the Senate struggle. Senator Hoar, who through his long, useful public career had been one of the most regular of Republicans, strenuously fought the treaty in the Senate despite his personal affection for McKinley. Henry Adams, who by

14. A. A. Berle in the Anti-Imperialist League's *Free America, Free Cuba, Free Philippines: Addresses at a Meeting in Faneuil Hall, Saturday, March 30, 1901* (Boston, 1901), 50–56; Charles Warren, *The Development of a Policy, and the Contradictions Which May Arise Therefrom: Extract from the Annual Report of the Massachusetts Reform Club for the Year 1899* [Boston, 1900], 14 pp. Warren was secretary of the Massachusetts Reform Club.

this time was experiencing misgivings about imperialism, wrote from Washington on January 29, 1899:

"Old Hoar is quite frantic. In executive session the other day he declared to the Senate that if he could only prevent the ratification of that Treaty, he would willingly lay his head upon the block before the Vice-President's chair. So Cabot told me with a gasp. I would gladly see the execution, on the same condition, if I could see how under the scaffold of this sainted man I could find an escape from the Philippines. *Nous y sommes*, and as far as I can see, Treaty or no Treaty, we must stay, and fight the Philippinos. No one wants it. Poor [Senator Eugene] Hale is at last whipped till he cowers. There is no fight left in him . . .

"Our army is in as bad a condition as the French. It needs complete reconstruction. . . . In case of serious operations in the Philippines, I really do not see a hope of escaping awful disaster. Of course we can thrash the Philippinos and kill them by the hundred thousand, but it will cost in one season at least fifty thousand men, fifty millions of money, and indefinite loss of reputation."[15]

Just before the treaty came to a vote, hostilities broke out between the American and Philippine forces. On the evening of February 4, 1899, American pickets shot three Filipinos who refused to halt, and within a few minutes the two forces arrayed against each other around Manila were in full battle. The next day, General Arthur MacArthur's forces began to push the Filipinos back, but Henry Adams' prediction was to come true—indeed fall far short of the mark.

15. Henry Adams to Elizabeth Cameron, Jan. 29, 1899, cited in W. C. Ford, ed., *Letters of Henry Adams (1892–1918)* (Boston, Houghton Mifflin, 1938), 209.

11. Uncle Sam uses American soldiers as darts in this cover cartoon in the satirical-political magazine *The Verdict* on June 19, 1899. The two little applauders are President McKinley (left) and the Republican leader Mark Hanna.

By a margin of only two votes, the Senate ratified the treaty. Roosevelt crowed to Lodge: "I am more grateful than I can say, partly to the Senate, partly to Providence and partly to the Filipinos. They just pulled the treaty through for us. As for your colleague [Hoar], he can be pardoned only on the ground that he is senile. His position is precisely that of the cotton whigs whom he so reprobated forty years ago."[16]

In point of fact, Hoar's position, as he and the anti-imperialists insisted through the long travail of the insurrection, was precisely the opposite. They were the self-conscious heirs to the Conscience Whigs who had so firmly opposed the Mexican War. Indeed, when news began to reach the United States of the cruelty with which the rebellion was being suppressed, they held the Philippine Insurrection to be even worse than the Mexican War. John White Chadwick, a Unitarian minister in Brooklyn, preached:

"Theodore Parker hated our war with Mexico with a perfect hatred because it was virtually a war for the extension of slavery and because it was initiated with a wicked lie. . . . But Theodore Parker said of that most wicked war—the darkest blot upon our national escutcheon until now—that it was conducted with conspicuous humanity. Can we say that of our war for the subjugation of Luzon?"[17]

As for Senator Hoar, who came so close to blocking the treaty, deserted by Bryan who advised Democrats to vote for it, and by all Republican Senators except Hale of Maine, he

16. Roosevelt to Lodge, Feb. 7, 1899. *Letters of Theodore Roosevelt*, II, 935.

17. J. W. Chadwick, *The Present Distress: A Sermon upon Our Oriental War* (New York, 1899), 17.

repeatedly harked back to the precepts of his revolutionary forebears. To Hale he gave a large engraving of the signing of the Declaration of Independence, noting on it that Hale was the only one of his Republican colleagues who had not voted for its repeal.

Perhaps the sharpest historical analogy was that which Charles Francis Adams, Jr., the president of the Massachusetts Historical Society, drew in a letter he sent to be read at a public meeting in Tremont Temple in April 1899. He said that in view of the "very gallant resistance the unfortunate Filipinos are making against our wholly unprovoked assault upon them," the situation was comparable to what it would have been:

". . . had our French allies, after the war of independence, accepted the colonies as a transfer from England, taken the war on their own shoulders, and proceeded, as we express it with the Filipinos, to 'subdue' the rebels, on the ground . . . that there was no evidence whatever that we were capable of governing ourselves; and the French, therefore, were responsible for us to their own consciences, and before God and the world,—and duty made destiny. Neither would there have been anything in the record of the next eight years under the old federation to have shown that they were not right in such a conclusion. On the contrary, Shays' rebellion in Massachusetts would have quite justified them in such course of reasoning and line of procedure."[18]

Edward Atkinson, an iconoclastic and resourceful veteran of many decades of pamphleteering wars, became a partic-

18. C. F. Adams, Jr., in the Anti-Imperialist League's *In the Name of Liberty: Anti-Imperialist Meeting, Tremont Temple, April 4, 1899; Protest Against Philippine Policy* (Boston, 1899), 31.

ularly keen thorn in the side of the administration. He began publishing a series of anti-imperialist pamphlets, containing not only the full array of conventional arguments, but also a lively additional section, "The Hell of War and its Penalties," detailing the susceptibility of troops stationed in the tropics to fevers, malaria, leprosy, and especially venereal disease. Each year, Atkinson asserted, half the British forces stationed in Hong Kong were infected with venereal disease. To save the morals, health, and lives of young men fighting in the Philippines, they should be ordered home. As for those in America, he suggested, "The way has already become plain for the youth of the land to avoid disease and death in the tropics by refusing to volunteer or to enlist in the army or navy of the United States."[19]

What made Atkinson particularly obnoxious to officials in Washington was his publicly proclaimed intention in April 1899 to distribute copies of his pamphlets among the armed forces in the Philippines. He wrote the Secretary of the Treasury, Lyman J. Gage, "In this morning's paper a correspondent of the Boston *Herald* states that the Departments are going to '*expose*' the Anti-Imperialist League and others who have as alleged stirred up discontent among the troops in Manila. I do not think the Executive Committee of the Anti-Imperialist League have yet taken any active measures to inform the troops of the facts and conditions there. The suggestion is, however, a valuable one and I have sent to Washington today to get specific addresses of officers and soldiers to the number of five hundred or six hundred so

19. Edward Atkinson, *The Anti-Imperialist* (Boston, 1899). Various revisions and new numbers of this appeared. See the first pamphlet (published May 27, 1899), 17–35.

that I may send them my pamphlets giving them assurance of sympathy."[20]

Atkinson, failing, of course, to receive lists, next created a flurry of excitement by mailing copies of the pamphlets to Admiral Dewey, General Ewell S. Otis, and several other prominent figures in the Philippines. The Postmaster General rose to the bait and ordered the offending pamphlets seized from the mail sacks in San Francisco. The national publicity that followed created a sharp demand for the pamphlets; altogether Atkinson distributed about 135,000 copies. In the fall of 1899, he wrote a pamphlet which he described as "my strongest bid yet for a limited residence in Fort Warren," but the McKinley administration did not again make the mistake of giving official notice to Atkinson.[21]

The anti-imperialists did stir up wrathful response from their opponents. Frederick Chamberlin, a lawyer who earlier had been Harvard correspondent for several Boston papers, and who later went on a special mission for the government to the Philippines, published a stinging attack:

"Just as we were in the hottest of our campaign against Aguinaldo which we were waging to protect the great mass of Filipinos and to meet our obligations . . . there struck our army over there . . . 'The blow from behind.'

"As if out of the ground, there arose in this country a set of people calling themselves anti-imperialists. They were first seen in Boston. These people said that if it were not for them, this republic would become an empire; and they had

20. Edward Atkinson to Lyman J. Gage, April 22, 1899, cited in H. F. Williamson, *Edward Atkinson: The Biography of an American Liberal, 1827–1905* (Boston, Old Corner Book Store, Inc., 1934), 228.

21. Beisner, *Twelve Against Empire*, 98–101.

come to prevent that. They said that if we kept on trying to save the Filipinos from Aguinaldo and anarchy, this republic would pass from the earth and an empire would rise in its stead. They took to print, and they flooded the mails with pamphlets called 'The Anti-Imperialist' . . .

"The high priest of this 'Anti-Imperialist' is Edward Atkinson of Boston, a gentleman, who, I believe, has secured the printing of more statistics with respect to matters that had nothing to do with his own vocation, which is, I am informed, that of fire insurance, than probably anybody else in the universe."

Then Chamberlin tore apart Atkinson's statistics on the cost of the war and predicted casualties, and heaped shame upon him because he "thrust before the loving eyes of the mothers, sisters and sweethearts of the 100,000 men we sent out there, prophecies that they can probably never forgive."[22]

If one were to believe the imperialists and the outraged American command in the Philippines, little else seemed to sustain the *insurrectos* but encouragement from American opponents of the war. The anti-imperialists counterattacked by charging the military authorities with censoring all news out of the Philippines which would reflect badly upon them or upon Washington.

That there was much to censor and withhold from the American public slowly became apparent as correspondents' dispatches became less enthusiastic and soldiers' private letters home began to make their way into the hands of the anti-imperialists. Though the soldiers may have exaggerated

22. F. C. Chamberlin, *The Blow from Behind or Some Features of the Anti-Imperialist Movement* . . . (Boston, 1903), 52–53.

12. The artist George B. Luks, associated with the "ash-can school" of American painting, depicts a war correspondent in the Philippines writing a dispatch under severe restraints by American generals including Ewell S. Otis. Mark Hanna (left) and President McKinley look on from their pictures on the wall. The cartoon was in *The Verdict* of August 21, 1899.

or indulged in tall tales, the fact was that the insurrection was turning into a cruel war, shocking in its savagery. The *insurrectos* had relatively few guns and did not know how to use them. They usually removed the rear sight, aimed only with the front sight, pulled the trigger hard, and sent their bullets flying well over the heads of the Americans, who, aiming carefully, slaughtered their foes by the hundreds and thousands. The *insurrectos*, after their initial defeats, resorted to guerrilla tactics, striking, then disappearing into an apparently peaceful countryside, where they were protected by villagers. They sometimes meted out fearful treatment upon captured Americans, burying them alive. As for the Americans, they resorted to no-quarter war, taking no prisoners, burning villages, at times gunning down men, women, and children. On one notorious occasion they shot up a wedding party. To elicit information from reluctant villagers they resorted to such Spanish techniques as the "water cure." This was the device of pouring water into the victim until he went through the sensations of drowning, then pumping him out, and if need be repeating the process. Others were hanged briefly to refresh their memories.

Before the end of 1899 the Anti-Imperialist League published several score of letters like this:

"The town . . . was surrendered to us a few days ago, and two companies occupy the same. Last night one of our boys was found shot and his stomach cut open. Immediately orders were received from [the] General . . . to burn the town and kill every native in sight, which was done to a finish. About one thousand men, women, and children were reported killed. I am probably growing hard-hearted, for I am

MAMA!

13. Philippine cat gives President McKinley more than he can handle while "second term" balloon escapes. From *The Verdict* of July 17, 1899. This and the other cartoons in this chapter appeared in the magazine in color.

in my glory when I can sight my gun on some dark-skin and pull the trigger."[23]

These allegations outraged the anti-imperialists, and led many of them in 1900 to support Bryan, despite their distaste for his "free silver" heresy, when he ran against McKinley for the second time. "There are worse things than financial troubles in a Nation's career," wrote William James. "To puke up its ancient soul, and the only things that gave it eminence among other nations, in five minutes without a wink of squeamishness, is worse; and that is what the Republicans would commit us to in the Philippines. Our con-

23. A. A. Barnes, Battery G., Third United States Artillery, writing about the town of Titatia in the Anti-Imperialist League's *Soldiers' Letters: Being Materials for the History of a War of Criminal Aggression* (Boston, 1899), 15. Barnes's letter has not been verified, and was doubtless an exaggeration, at least in its report of a thousand deaths. In response to American protests, military officials in the Philippines sought to refute many such letters, and obtained written recantations from the enlisted men who were their authors. Private Edward E. Baker thus stated that he had written home that they shot Filipinos like rabbits mainly in order to amuse his parents and show them that he was not in great danger. The command indignantly refuted the story of the shooting into a wedding party, killing the bride and wounding the groom, which former Governor John P. Altgeld of Illinois had quoted from a private's letter. Major S. W. Miller reported, "The casualties were 2 men and 1 woman dead, 1 woman and 2 children wounded, all natives, and found in the building. The gathering in the house was no doubt that of a celebration or feast of some kind, most probably a wedding, but I could find no evidence that the bride had been killed or the bridegroom wounded in the unfortunate occurrence." Moreover, reported Major Miller, the officers had sought to restrain the enlisted men from shooting into the building. Major General J. C. Bates commented, "This matter seems to have been grossly exaggerated in the newspaper report, and the occurrence, deplorable as it is, seems to have been due to armed insurrectos mingling with a festive gathering." U.S., War Dept., *Charges of Cruelty, etc., to the Natives of the Philippines* (57 Cong., 1 Sess., Sen. Doc. no. 205, part 1, 1902), 13, 17–18.

14. At right, cartoon from *The Verdict* of August 27, 1900.

CITIZEN OR SUBJECT—WHICH?

"DO I REPRESENT THE IDEA OF POPULAR GOVERNMENT TO TEN MILLION OF THESE, OR AM I SIMPLY A TRADEMARK FOR GOODS OF AMERICAN TRUST MANUFACTURE?"

duct there has been one protracted infamy towards the Islanders, and one protracted lie towards ourselves."[24]

The American electorate did not agree. As a matter of fact, not all the anti-imperialists agreed, and many of the most prominent Republicans among them put party first and did not concentrate their energies publicly to try to defeat McKinley. Even in their New England stronghold, the anti-imperialists won only one petty victory. That came in the spring of 1901 when indignant Harvard alumni, hearing that McKinley was to receive an honorary degree, signed a manifesto expressing their opposition. Senator Hoar, who was president of the Harvard Alumni, tried in vain to stop the movement, and McKinley to avoid embarrassment declined the invitation to attend the commencement.

As the war against the *insurrectos* dragged on into 1901 and 1902, the anti-imperialists gained a public hearing by their continued protestations against the atrocities. Elihu Root became Secretary of War and began to look into the evidence that Charles Francis Adams submitted to him. The resulting hearings uncovered much that was unsavory: savage conduct which, when it occasionally led to courts-martial, resulted only in trivial punishment. For example, two officers were tried for "wilfully and cruelly causing six Filipinos to be hung by the neck for a period of ten seconds, causing them to suffer great bodily pain." The court changed the charge from "great bodily pain" to "mental anguish," found the officers guilty, and sentenced them to reprimands. It should be added that General MacArthur disapproved of the court's light sentence.[25]

24. William James to Henry Lee Higginson, Sept. 18, 1900, cited in Bliss Perry, *Life and Letters of Henry Lee Higginson* (2 vols., Boston, Atlantic Monthly Press, 1921), II, 429.

25. U.S., War Dept., *Trials or Courts-Martial in the Philippine Islands in*

By the time these disgraceful matters had been aired in Washington, the Philippine Insurrection was over. It had dragged on for three years, had cost more American lives than the Spanish-American War and perhaps as many as two hundred thousand Filipino lives. The dissenters in the United States had utterly failed to stop it. Once they had lost the treaty fight, the war seemed to go on automatically under the control of the military leaders. Other issues splitting the nation were more important to voters; in 1900 the election seemed less a referendum on the Philippine Insurrection than on McKinley's "full dinnerpail." There seemed no way to curb the military.

Yet in other respects, the dissenters were somewhat less than complete failures. They had called national attention to the horrors of the Insurrection, and were particularly successful in doing so after the election, in 1901–1902. In the end they brought about a considerable degree of national revulsion, and in consequence an end to this sort of imperialist venture. There were to be further interventions during the Progressive Era—in the Caribbean, Central America, and even Mexico—but never on the scale of the Philippines. The thirst for additional colonies had suddenly and permanently been slaked. There was not to be the grandiose building of empire that some jingoes had hoped would be America's future. Indeed, the consensus seemed to have shifted to

---

Consequence of Certain Instructions (57 Cong., 2 Sess., Sen. Doc. no. 213, 1903), 92–97; U.S. Senate, Committee on the Philippines, *Affairs in the Philippine Islands* (57 Cong., 2 Sess., Sen. Doc. no. 331, 1903), 901–906. The court-martial was held June 4, 1900. For a selection of testimony from the 1902 hearings, see H. G. Graff, ed., *American Imperialism and the Philippine Insurrection . . .* (Boston, Little, Brown, 1969). For an over-all account of the Philippine Insurrection, see Leon Wolff, *Little Brown Brother: How the United States Purchased and Pacified the Philippine Islands at the Century's Turn* (Garden City, N.Y., Doubleday, 1961).

15. *The Verdict*'s opinion of what the American troops in the Philippines were doing. The cartoon appeared September 17, 1900. Notice McKinley at upper left.

the view that ultimately, when they were ready, the Filipinos must have their independence.[26]

The Philippine Insurrection, like other unpopular wars, raised the question whether or not objectors should have the right to dissent. One of those who commented most interestingly upon this question at the time was Mark Twain. He had responded with vigorous horror to suppression of the Filipinos, bitterly writing that the American flag should have "the white stripes painted black and the stars replaced by the skull and crossbones." A short while later he heard a clergyman publicly attack him. "He said that if I had my just deserts I should be . . . dangling from a lamp-post somewhere . . . He hadn't anything personal against me, except that I was opposed to the political war, and he said I was a traitor." Then Twain insisted, "It would be an entirely different question if the country's life was in danger, its existence at stake; then . . . we would all come forward and stand by the flag, and stop thinking about whether the nation was right or wrong; but when there is no question that the nation is any way in danger, but only some little war away off, then it may be that on the question of politics the nation is divided, half-patriot and half-traitors, and no man can tell which from which."[27]

26. For an account of continuing efforts of the anti-imperialists to gain freedom for the Philippines, see the study by Moorfield Storey, one of the most prominent and persistent of their number, and Marcial P. Lichauco, *The Conquest of the Philippines by the United States, 1898–1925* (New York, Putnam's, 1926).

27. Mark Twain, speaking at the Lotos Club, March 23, 1901, in John Elderkin *et al.*, eds., *After Dinner Speeches at the Lotos Club* (New York, 1911), 14–15.

Index